UNIVERSITAS NUE

How can we begin to create a new civilization?

Luis Razeto Migliaro.

Author:
Luis Razeto Migliaro.

First Edition:
Edition Uvirtual.net, Santiago of Chile, 2011.

Intellectual property registration:
N° 211.240

Front:
Walter Ziller R.

Traslate in English:
Lafayette Claud Eaton Henderson

Digital Edition:
UNIVERSITAS NUEVA CIVILIZACIÓN, Santiago of Chile, 2013.

I.

In which it is proposed that modern civilization is in crisis and the need to create a new civilization is formulated.

Throughout history and in different parts of the world many civilizations with different features have been created. Civilizations have been of various sizes; some very large, others small. Real people have created them, men and women like us, through activities and theoretical and practical processes that we can identify through the study of history.

If we look beyond the differences between them, we can learn quite clearly what a civilization is, its foundations and its pillars, its main structures and the elements that shape it. And we can also discover when a civilization declines and tends to disappear, how and when the need to create a new civilization arises, and what are the initiatives and activities deployed by what kind of people and groups that begin its creation.

All this knowledge about past civilizations, applied to the present reality, allows us to say that we are living today a historical phase in which our civilization is in organic crisis and has started to decay, while the initiatives and activities tending to create a superior civilization begin to unfold to replace it.

The historical knowledge of past civilizations and of the present modern civilization, from its inception, development, consolidation and crisis, can greatly facilitate the theoretical and practical action of those who today intend to lay the foundations and begin the creation of a new and superior civilization that will open human experience to new and broader horizons.

In this small volume I propose to synthesize all these ideas and to express them in an accessible language to anyone who may be interested.

The need to build a new civilization is felt by many, with varying degrees of understanding of what it is and what it means. This need has been raised by many intellectuals for several decades, and the concept has been adopted by different types of groups and organizations.

We may formulate the situation in these terms: The present modern civilization is in an organic crisis and the three pillars or foundations that support it are also in crisis. Its political pillar is in crisis, including the (sovereign) state and parties; the economic pillar, including industrialism and capitalism is in crisis; and its cultural pillar, including ideologies, social sciences, and positivistic ethics is also in crisis.

These three dimensions of the crisis are evident because of their multiple effects, which we can summarize in the exhaustion of a mode of economic development, of forms of civil and political coexistence, and of some ideological and theoretical paradigms that are incapable of making sense of life in society or proposing viable solutions to the major problems of society that are worsening.

The fact that the fundamental pillars (economic, political and cultural) are all in crisis indicates that modern civilization is showing its exhaustion and its inability to continue contributing to the expansion and improvement of human experience.

However, our purpose here is not to analyze the crisis but to inquire about the **ways, initiatives and options through which it is possible to start creating a new civilization superior to the one in which we live.**

Since these crises are organic, they can be solved only by a new organization, because as any organism whose vital foundations are in great crisis, modern civilization and its pillars are doomed to continue deteriorating. However, this progressive decline is very slow and the process can be extended for the next few decades, even though there are clear signs that the economic, political and cultural crises are accelerating.

Faced with these crises we have two possibilities (if we want to do something socially useful); one is to try to shore up, strengthen and improve the pillars of the civilization in crisis so that the collapse may be postponed for a while, reducing thus the suffering that the crises bring and the collapse itself will bring. The other possibility is to start building the foundations of a new, superior civilization.

Issues such as reforming political parties, creating new and better parties, etc., belong in the first perspective. Improving income distribution and raising environmental requirements for new industrial developments is also an approach in the perspective of reinforcing the pillars of this civilization and thus delaying its fall. Those who do sociological research designed to increase knowledge about public opinion and to improve social policies are also in functioning in this perspective.

If instead we set our sights on the second perspective, that is, to initiate the creation of a new civilization, the essential issues are the creation of a new policy (non-partisan, non-state) of a new economy (not industrialist, non-capitalist), and new structures of knowledge and projection (non-ideological, non-positivist).

But there are many things implied in these statements, which must be examined more deeply. For now I have raised the issue, which I will expand and develop in the following chapters.

II.

Explaining what a civilization is and how there are important elements of continuity between one civilization and another.

I have posed the need to start creating a new civilization, since I demonstrated the crisis and decay of modern civilization. But what do we understand as a 'new civilization'?

The concepts which we can postulate for a new civilization superior to the current modern civilization will be identified and expounded progressively in this volume.

To begin, we may preliminarily indicate some of the elements and characteristics that shape what is meant by a 'civilization'. In general terms, a civilization is characterized by the diffusion of a lifestyle that involves the adoption of certain ways of thinking, feeling, behaving, acting and relating, which are spread among large groups of people. In this sense we say that each civilization forms and disseminates a characteristic 'human type'.

More specifically, a civilization is distinguished – in terms of the expression and social way of life that characterize it - by a certain way of doing and organizing economic activities. This includes a wide variety of issues such as our own way of experiencing needs, producing goods and services to satisfy them, distributing them among the diverse individuals and groups that are part of society, consuming and using the goods and services, developing and building what is needed to ensure the future, etc. And the base of this, implicitly, is a particular mode of processing and structuring relationships between socially organized individuals and the environment in which they are inserted.

A civilization is also characterized by the way it establishes and ensures social order, by the institutions that regulate the behaviors that are recognized as legitimate, meritorious and acceptable, that is, by a way of doing and organizing political life. All this is based on a particular mode of relationship between rulers and ruled, between those who direct and those who are directed, that is, a particular institutional order, actively or passively legitimized and socially accepted.

A civilization is also characterized by the ideas and values that govern, guide and give meaning to individual and social life; by the knowledge structures used in the understanding of reality and in the design of actions and changes that drive the subjects; by the values and ethics that govern the behavior recognized as meritorious; the forms assumed by art and intellectual creativity and aesthetics; in short, by the form and content adopted by the culture. The basis of all, implicitly or explicitly, is a particular mode of relationship between theory and practice, between knowledge and action.

This simple and concise presentation of what is a civilization and of all that it implies may cause us to despair, thinking that the creation of a new civilization implies such a radical change and such gigantic tasks and projects that these are beyond our reach. It is therefore important to make two clarifications.

The first is that this characterization of what a civilization is corresponds to its mature and consolidated structure, to a civilization fully and integrally formed; that is why it seems so enormous and therefore inaccessible. But what we need to do now is only to "start" the creation of a new civilization, give it a beginning, lay the groundwork for a process which will need to be continued for a long time before its consolidation, as has happened in all previous civilizations.

The second point concerns what a 'new' civilization really means. When one thinks of a 'new civilization', one tends to assume that it is a socio-economic-political-cultural order entirely different from the existing one, as if between one civilization and the next there must be a complete historical rupture.

This assumption stems from a mistaken view of what the decline of a civilization entails that might be called 'catastrophist', as if it should crumble like an entire building collapsing on its foundations. There is also a tendency to emphasize the elements of originality and distinction of each civilization from the previous one, in the process of identifying the traits and characteristics of each. Furthermore, the idea has spread that civilizations are like individuals; that they are born, grow old and die. Using this analogy, it is thought that each civilization is a different historical 'individual'; an old man dies, a child is born.

This conception of civilizations and the transition from one to another creates confusion, and is not what has happened historically. It is true that in human history there have been

9

cases of civilizations that disappeared completely, so that others have had to emerge with very little continuity with the previous one, creating a completely original social order. But this, which was more common in antiquity when social upheaval, environmental cataclysms, plagues and wars could destroy entire civilizations, has been disappearing. In more recent times, especially in the case of more widespread and strong civilizations, the elements of the preceding civilization that are conserved and which continue and are incorporated in the next civilization are increasing. What is lost is less than what is retrieved in the civilization which follows.

Thus it will be important, along with identifying the new and emerging foundations of a civilization to be built, to discover the elements of continuity; to understand what is conserved from the previous civilization, how it continues and remains active, and how this interacts with the decisive and original elements of the new civilization.

We will gradually examine these important issues in greater depth in the succeeding chapters.

III.

Here is identified the initiator subject of the new civilization, and is explained the "fetishism" of organizations.

The need for a new civilization is something that has been argued for some time. But little has been said about how to make it really happen. If, as explained above, a new civilization implies a new way of life, and the formation of a new 'human type', we must answer this question: how can we make way for the emergence of a new way of life and the formation of a new 'human type"?

I also affirmed that a new civilization involves creating and deploying a new economics, a new politics and a new culture. Thus we also need to address what the new economics, politics and culture can be and how they can be created. All this we will examine step by step.

The first question that arises when thinking about beginning to create a new civilization refers to **the subject**, the **actor** or **protagonist** of this remarkable project. In sociology, political science and the reformist and revolutionary ideologies it is often argued that the subject who can produce a process of social and political change is a collective subject, that is, a social class, political party, movement or social organization.

Contradicting this idea, when it comes to **start** creating a new civilization, I affirm that the individual is the first subject; that the **initiator** of the creation of a new civilization cannot be other than the individual, the human being that is going to inhabit it.

To say this does not deny that people who take on the project of the new civilization will have to associate, organize and interact with others, resulting in various types of collective entities (associations, communities, networks, etc.), which will reinforce the action and creative activity of the individuals themselves. But the individual will always be the primary subject. First the individuals must be identified, and only then you can see what and how these social formations will have to be, which will obviously be different from those that characterize the present civilization in crisis.

Identifying the individual as the subject who initiates a new civilization is of fundamental importance and is a significant novelty of the proposed creation of a new civilization with respect to the projects of political reform or social change within the civilization we are leaving behind. Indeed, modern civilization **has become** a civilization of organizations, a civilization of multiple struggles and conflicts, large corporations, political parties and mass social movements.

We say that modern civilization "has become" like this, because in fact originally it was also created by a certain type of individuals, specifically by individuals who saw themselves as subjects with political rights (i.e., no longer subjects of a king but citizens), as subjects with economic interests and incentives (such as entrepreneurs and businessmen), as subjects of free thought and cultural activity ('thinkers', intellectuals, artists, scientists, etc.). Also in the origin of modern civilization we find individuals who gave rise to a 'civil society' separate and independent from the traditional powers and institutions (feudal, monarchical, ecclesiastical, etc.), inherent to medieval civilization.

Modern civilization was a great and unique historical creation, which along with the emergence of the modern individual made possible the deployment of freedom of economic initiative, of social organization, of thought. This happened because, as I will discuss in detail later, civilization is initiated by the emergence of a 'human type' represented initially by a few people which then becomes more widespread.

Modern society has become so based on massive organizations that it is hard to think that the primary subject of so vast a change as a new civilization can be due to individuals. Currently there is what we might call a 'fetish' of organizations, in that a mythical value is attributed to them; organizations are conceived as meta-empirical entities that act even if their members are passive; which have science and historical knowledge even though they have no scientists and perform no scientific research, which are endowed with a culture and ideology even if its members do not engage in creative activities and do not share the same ideological convictions. It is believed that organizations are able to intervene effectively in history in spite of the specific theoretical and practical activities of its members.

13

Antonio Gramsci said about this 'fetishism': "A collective organism is made up of individuals, which form the organism by giving and actively accepting a hierarchy and a given leadership. If each of the individuals thinks of the collective organism as an entity external to himself or herself, it is clear that the organism as such ceases to exist and becomes a ghost of the intellect, a fetish. This is common to a number of organisms, including the State, nation, political parties, etc. One tends to think of the relationship between the individual and the organization as a dualism, and to have a critical exterior attitude of the individual towards the organism (unless the attitude is enthusiastic and uncritical admiration), which in any case is a fetishistic relationship. The individual expects the agency to act, even though she or he does not act, and does not reflect that if this passive attitude is widespread, the organism will be inoperative."

What Gramsci is observing is that the subject of the action is always the individual, even in the case of 'social' action or historical action. Communities are formed by people, who are the only ones that can act, while the 'collective subject' moves only to the extent that the individual subjects move. The direction a collective movement takes will always be the result of a combination of the actions of the individuals within it.

What is causing the 'fetishism' of organizations? In reality in modern society they are based on a clear separation between leaders and led; thus organizations create centers of power and bureaucratic structures, which in fact act because its members act. However, the great majority of the led remain inactive, and they endure the results of the action of the leaders. Thus, as a way to hide the relationship of power and domination configured in this way, the action of the powerful is attributed to the institutions and organizations, which are thus 'fetishized' for the mass of subordinates subjected to them, unaware that they are subordinating themselves to individuals and special groups.

Naturally, this fetishism of organizations and institutions must be overcome in order for a new civilization to arise, because the individuals who create it must recover for themselves the role of decisions and action. From this affirmation of the individual as a first subject who originates a new civilization, a statement that we will have to analyze further, we draw a first conclusion: each of us can become protagonist of the creation of a civilization which is new and superior to the existing one.

IV.

Noting that the new civilization is already being built by creative, autonomous and solidary people.

In the previous section I asked what is the primary subject, actor and protagonist in the creation of a new civilization, and responded by saying that it can only be individuals, men and women. Collective entities cannot be initiators of a new civilization unless they have already appeared previously, composed of people who are carriers of the modes of being, thinking, relating and acting of this new civilization.

However, the individual subject-initiators of the new civilization will not be the men and women who are perfectly adapted to the civilization that perishes. The vast majority of contemporary women and men are people shaped by the standards of the modern civilization in crisis. Obviously the founders of a new and higher civilization cannot be from the mass of individuals who are consumers, fashion followers, competitive, social climbers; those who are dependent on the 'system' and subordinate to the modes of feeling, of relating and of behavior which respond to the requirements and demands of modern economics, politics and culture.

In an article in which I discussed in a series of videos under the title: "Needs and human nature (in the context of the question of the possibility of a higher civilization)" I examined the conditions which underlie the possibility of formation and development of a 'new human type'; people able to begin creating a new civilization by being carriers of this new incipient behavior in their modes of living, relating, behaving and acting. Here I take the positive answer found in this examination as existing, that is the claim that human beings can configure themselves in different and varied ways, and therefore the emergence of new ways of being individuals, of being human beings, men and women is possible.

Now I will advance a general characterization of the 'human type' needed to start creating a new civilization superior to the existing one. We can identify and characterize this type as an individual, man or woman, who is **creative, autonomous and solidary.** Why creative? Why autonomous? Why solidary? We will examine each of these aspects as we proceed in our analysis and reflections.

I can and must state now, to avoid what would be a grave mistake, that whatever we mean by a 'creative, independent and solidary' person must necessarily be a way of being human that needs to be made, constructed, developed, from the way of being of real people living in this decaying civilization. No one can 'form' or 'build' or deploy it externally. It is necessary for the individual to form himself or herself, freely and voluntarily, experiencing personally the process of becoming a creative, independent and solidary individual. This means, more specifically, that the current real people who want to be creators of a new civilization **must develop their creativity, gain their autonomy and learn to be solidary** through a process of personal development.

This personal development cannot be imposed from the outside on each person, individual, but may be facilitated and supported by others who, more advanced in achieving these qualities of creativity, autonomy and solidarity, open the way, bear witness and show that it is possible, and offer them the results of their own progress and achievements on which others can rely. Later I will examine the importance of education and communication in this process.

That said, I affirm that creative, autonomous and solidary people already exist, and probably to a greater extent than is commonly believed. This means that **a new civilization superior to that in crisis is already here among us as a germ, a seed.** And if this is so, the first thing to do is to **learn to recognize it, discover it, and resolve to participate in its development**.

It is obvious that the construction of a new civilization is a gigantic project, task, labor. But history shows that the beginning of a civilization is something that happens with some spontaneity. If we look at the great civilizations that have occurred throughout human history, in fact we find that their beginnings were usually processes implemented by a few people, based on a specific set of very clear and deep ideas, never complicated or difficult to understand.

In fact, new civilizations begin to appear within civilizations in organic crisis, in which the construction of a new superior civilization appears as a necessity, and in response to real and current issues affecting the lives of people. This need is felt at first by a few people, and some responses to situations that occur are initially faced by small groups. But awareness of this need and the initiatives deployed initially on a small scale spread very rapidly as the crisis of the old civilization is accentuated, deteriorating civil life, harmony, quality of life, the values and ideas that sustained it for centuries, which will mean very little to future generations.

As I said, civilizations have always begun with the labors and actions of a few individuals and the small groups that they themselves created, which gradually expanded due to the integration of a growing number of participants to be a significant intellectual, moral and political force. That is, **the new civilization emerges in the midst of the current civilization and will live together with it for a long time.**

We can say that the new civilization already exists, at a very small scale, when the first group or set of individuals forms who live, interact, think, feel and behave in the manner and content of the civilization being built.

I say with full conviction that a new civilization is already building, that many people are actually participating in it, and that in different parts of the world they are laying the foundation on which it will stand as a great social construction.

Obviously, not every individual who claims to be the bearer of a new civilization is really an embryo and initiator of a new civilization. Those individuals and groups who deserve to be called founders must meet certain conditions, without which they can never be spread to cover the necessary dimensions of a civilization.

In general terms, they must carry the seed, the essential components of the new, superior civilization. They must be, as mentioned, creative, autonomous and solidary individuals and groups. We will examine what each of these terms implies in the following sections.

V.

In this it's beginning to explain the meaning of the necessary autonomy and show that it is not easy to achieve.

I affirmed that the actors and players in the creation of a new civilization are creative, autonomous and solidary people; three words that characterize the distinctive 'human type' of a superior civilization. I will define the meaning and implications of each of these concepts.

Let us begin with autonomy, a necessary condition that the individuals who begin a new civilization should have, because anyone who is dependent or subordinate or who is somehow trapped in the given civilization cannot be active in creating a new one.

As a first approximation we can say that to be autonomous one must think with one's own mind and make one's own decisions, and not delegate decisions about the most important aspects that affect our lives. Autonomous people are individuals who have decided for themselves to recover control over their own living conditions.

How to achieve autonomy, think with our own mind, decide for ourselves, regain control of our living conditions is not easy or obvious. Many people believe themselves to be autonomous, since they feel they live as they want to live and have their lives under control, but in fact they behave according to the dictates of the group to which they belong. Their aspirations are no different from those of the majority; they adhere to most of the ideas given by the media, consume what advertising says they should, follow the current fashions of clothing and goods, wish to have their homes in the places that everyone thinks are the most prestigious, try to have their children study in educational institutions that appear in the rankings as the best, go into debt in the banking system, have fun at the entertainment centers where many people go, take their vacations in places that advertisers say they will enjoy, take care of their jobs as do their neighbors and coworkers, act as they have been taught they must to keep their job, prestige and membership in their groups, read books that are recommended by the usual critics or are best sellers, and see the most popular films.

Those who have credit card debts with stores or in the financial system are far from being autonomous, at least as far as the time it would take them to be free of all indebtedness incurred by following the patterns of consumption and expenditure that the system" wants them to follow, which forces them to pursue as a permanent objective the money necessary to cover the monthly bills. Obviously it is the creditors who are responsible for this; they are the ones who induced the person to go into debt by adopting these consumption patterns and this lifestyle.

We will discuss economic and political dependence and possible ways to overcome them later; first we must discuss the most difficult and important aspect, cultural autonomy, which begins with **thinking with our own mind**.

Antonio Gramsci, an Italian philosopher whom I consider to be a precursor and in some ways the founder of the science of history and politics oriented to lay the foundations of a new civilization, said that to get to think independently, one must first become aware that what we usually do is take part mechanically in worldviews we have passively acquired or learned in school, in the Church, in political parties, in the media, in the market. He said that normally we adopt ideas and ways of thinking and feeling uncritically, "naturally", borrowing from social groups in which we were born or into which we integrate at different times in our lives, and that permeate our consciousness without us really realizing it. Thus we accept the "common sense" which we absorb from certain groups, certain cultures, from a given civilization. For example, we think of ourselves as integrated into a nation, we believe in a State which we expect to solve many problems, we adhere to certain political ideologies, we adopt certain religious, ethical and philosophical beliefs, which we have not personally created and which we have not subjected to reflection and criticism.

This does not mean that those ideas and beliefs are all false or erroneous or negative, only that we have not elaborated them personally, we passively assume them, we adopted them just as they were presented to us. The problem is that by configuring our consciousness in this way we acquired a heterogeneous and confused thinking, since the ideas that we adopt have been received and continue arriving from many sources.

To get to think for ourselves, at the level of autonomy required to be creators of a new civilization, Gramsci suggested that an essential requirement must be to make a critical re-view of all our beliefs, even the most fundamental.

Subjecting them to criticism does not mean to discard our beliefs, deny them or abandon them. Rather, it means to work on them and **take them to a superior level of processing, integrate them into a unitary construct, attain a higher viewpoint from which we can understand the historical significance of the different theories, ideologies and beliefs.**

Gramsci wrote: "To criticize one's conception of the world is to render it conscious and homogeneous, and raise it to the level that now is the world's most advanced thinking." He added: "The beginning of critical elaboration is the consciousness of what we really are, that is to "know thyself" as a product of the historical process that has left in you countless traces received without benefit of an inventory. We must begin to make that inventory." This means to recognize the origins of our beliefs and ideas we have adopted, and then, considering what we have learned and accepted as only a starting point, create, innovate and develop our own thinking.

Sure, this seems too difficult, very complex almost unattainable. But nobody said that beginning the creation of a new civilization would be easy. In addition, of course, no one can do it alone. Thus the importance that from the beginning of the creation of the new civilization, those who propose it as a goal, who wish to collaborate in such an important project and who aspire to independence must interact, associate, discuss, criticize each other and cooperate in the process of accessing the superior point of view. **Progressing towards autonomy is also simultaneously a way of increasing solidarity.**

VI.

I reject confrontational anti-system concepts, and explain the stages and modes of the conquest of autonomy.

To understand correctly the meaning of the cultural autonomy needed to move towards the creation of a new civilization, we must clearly differentiate countercultural proposals and political antagonists against the capitalist and state "system".

There are, I believe, two fundamental limitations of these critical approaches. The first is that they remain within a left-wing conception (socialist, Marxist, neo-Marxist) which is part of the current political system of the civilization of state and party, and think that capitalism will be overcome as a result a struggle against the system, and therefore they require the existence of anti-system political subjects, antagonists, fighters, revolutionaries.

The other limit of these antagonistic conceptions is the assumption that the 'system' is so powerful and able to co-opt and control everything that nothing can be created that transcends it until it is first destroyed. This indicates a lack of understanding of the potential of intellectual and moral autonomy that can be achieved by creative, autonomous and solidary individuals, self-organized groups who, based on that creativity, autonomy and solidarity, can start creating a new superior civilization without having to first destroy capitalism and statism.

It is very important to understand in depth the essential distinction between antagonism and autonomy, which is crucial and novel, since most of the proposals of social, political and economic change are currently understood in the sense of a struggle 'against' the system, i.e., in terms of antagonism and not of autonomy; we must understand why acting like that is sterile and does not contribute – and often even makes it harder - to create a new civilization.

We will examine this beginning with an idea proposed by Gramsci, according to which to achieve autonomy a cultural, social or political movement must go beyond certain phases or primitive stages of development.

A first event or phase is a split, break or separation, i.e., a differentiation, separation and 'break' with the reality of the current system, which along with rejecting the system establishes a personal identity; however, this is identity defined as a negation of and reaction to the existing reality. For example, in the case capitalism it would be non-capitalist, or simply the proposal of a non-capitalist project. This stage is perhaps necessary, but will not produce results and achievements, because separating from the given reality and not interacting with it does not transform the reality, and the person becomes an isolated island.

A second phase is antagonism, that is, opposition, contradiction and fighting the existing reality which one wants to deny, destroy, or overcome. Personal identity at this stage is defined by opposition; it is an identity "against", or "anti"; for example, being anti-capitalist and deciding to fight against capitalism. In this type of movement one interacts with the general reality, but in the form of struggle and conflict, and the result cannot go beyond the development of the conflict itself. The adversary is reinforced in proportion to the intensity of the struggle of those who fight and a new reality is not generated, except for the exacerbation of antagonism.

These two moments or phases, or rather, the movements that have these levels of consciousness and proposals are not autonomous, because they are defined in terms of what they criticize, and therefore remain subordinate to it. Opposition, criticism, antagonism, the fight against, are attitudes that remain at the level of denial of the old, not the affirmation of the superior new, they do not even manage to conceive or to project, because at that stage consciousness remains within the existing reality in terms of which people define themselves as opposites, enemies and combatants.

Achieving autonomy implies going beyond denial and antagonism, requiring a positive self-definition based on your own superior, comprehensive view of the world (and your cultural, political, economic project).

Autonomy should be clearly distinguished from split or rupture, and this is not always understood, because one tends to think of autonomy as independence, as differentiation and as diversity. Gramsci says, however, that autonomy is access to a superior, higher point of view, which we have called 'comprehensive'. We must reach a higher position "inaccessible to the enemy camp." The idea is not to leave and stay **out** (separation) or to be **against** (antagonism), but **to rise above**, in the sense of reaching a broader view, and be able to value even the "adversaries" and learn from them, and make them part of the process itself, without fear of being absorbed by them.

In primitive phases (or movements) of disruption and antagonism the enemy, the "system", is feared, and above all there is the fear of being reabsorbed by it, since it is imagined to possess a superior strength. Thus in this phase the main intellectual activity is criticism, the denial of opposing views, a criticism which tends to be total and complete, because it is believed that if one accepts or recognizes an element of truth, validity or value in the system, it is feared that those criticized views may 'infiltrate', contaminate, or that followers will get caught and be co-opted, or at least the antagonism and conflict is weakened.

By contrast, in the stage of autonomy there is no fear of the enemy, because in reality you do not have an opponent, only little-developed concepts that must be superseded. We should and must integrate into our own superior concepts, knowledge and projects everything that can be discovered to be true and valuable in the previous reality and conceptions (which obviously cannot be totally wrong, null and of no value).

Even more important is the fact that the antagonistic movements refuse to create a new reality, or do not intend to start it in the present, because they believe that before the creation of the new, the old should be eliminated, the established system must collapse. And since it does not collapse, the years, decades and centuries pass in an endless struggle, and always with the hope of the collapse that has not come. Thus the creation of the new is always postponed.

But even worse is the fact that maintaining the antagonism, struggle and conflict has the predictable result of strengthening the "system" that the antagonists want to suppress because its defenders protect it against those who criticize and try to destroy it by force, reinforcing the system, refining it and so on.

To become autonomous, that is, to overcome moments of rupture or separation and antagonism, and then to raise oneself to a higher, understanding point of view, is a condition to initiate the creation of the new civilization. This creation should not expect the collapse of civilization to open the way and begin to spread its own potential.

VII.

Here is presented the second quality that distinguishes the 'human type' of the new civilization: solidarity.

I identify the individual creator of a new civilization as a 'human type' with three essential qualities; creativity, solidarity and autonomy. Men and women who are creators of a higher civilization are creative, autonomous and solidary people.

I referred above to autonomy, characterizing its main significance, distinguishing it from erroneous or inadequate ways of understanding and indicating the process through which we can achieve it. We now address solidarity, which also needs to be clearly identified and distinguished from wrong ways of understanding; it also requires a process of personal development to be achieved.

Solidarity -like autonomy- is a necessary condition that the subjects who start a new civilization must have, because a person who is individualistic or dedicated to her or his own interests cannot be active in the realization of a major human and social action that supposes the convergent and coordinated action toward goals shared by many people.

But we must clarify the meaning of the necessary solidarity, because currently, especially in the context of the current crisis of culture and politics, solidarity is often used frivolously, attributing traits to it that have little to do with authentic solidarity. Etymologically the word solidarity comes from the Latin word **'solidus'**, which has three meanings: 1. Solid, or firm, dense and strong. 2. A solid body, due to the high cohesion of the molecules, which maintains a constant volume. 3. A solid, consistent person, established with fundamental and true reasons.

Dictionaries include the following definitions of the word solidarity: 1.A link between several individuals together to collaborate and assist each other to meet needs. 2. All the links that unite the individual person with the community of which he/she forms part, and this with each individual person. 3. Human social solidarity is to share feelings, opinions, problems and pains with others and act accordingly.

We can say then, that in its original and rigorous meaning solidarity is a **horizontal relationship between people who form a group, association or a community** in which **participants are equal**. This interpersonal relationship or link is solidarity because of the strength **or intensity of mutual cohesion**, which must be more than the simple recognition that we all belong to a community. Solidarity implies an **especially committed, determined link, enduring over time**, which is manifested in effective action.

This strong and committed content that the word solidarity has is hidden in the frivolous use that has become common in many media, which in turn echoes the use and abuse it has in some social, religious and political groups. Indeed, it has become common to use the word solidarity to refer to assistance and charitable donations, as well as certain tax policies to provide subsidies to the poor and certain groups of disabled, handicapped or marginal people.

Such uses of the word change and to a certain degree distort and degrade the sense of solidarity, stripping it of five main contents of its original meaning: a) the strength of group interaction that leads to establish the fact or reality of solidarity as a solid body (something consistent, dense, that is not liquid, fluid or gaseous), b) equality of status and commitment or obligations found in are people who are caring and supportive c) the relationship among all with a bond of mutuality, reciprocity and participation in a group or community (made up of those who are solidary and supportive), d) the intensity of the mutual union which makes the group something strong, defined, established by fundamental and true reasons; e) the stable (not occasional) and permanent character of supportive cohesion.

Understanding solidarity in this demanding sense, we realize that becoming supportive is not easy, especially due to the current situation in which being individualistic, dedicating oneself to the achievement of personal interests, competing with others to climb to positions of prestige, power and wealth seem to be the basis of self-recognition and recognition of a person by others as successful, important and worthy of esteem and consideration.

The objective of initiating the creation of a new civilization thus implies the need for a personal development process, which must be simultaneous and convergent with the above-mentioned process of conquest of autonomy. However, while in the case of autonomy we emphasized that this is a process that must be deployed primarily by each individual, other people being contributors and facilitators of the personal process, in this case we invert the terms.

This is because solidarity, being a quality that may characterize an individual and distinguish him or her from others who are not, is however a quality that is formed, grows and becomes part of the relationship between people in their joint activities, in the process of formation of families, communities, organizations and networks. You cannot just be supportive or caring alone, only together with others. It is by being an integral part of these groups that we learn to be supportive, when within them we share objectives and form this consciousness, willingness and those shared and common feelings which constitute solidarity.

That said, it is important to understand that becoming solidary is not a process of denying one's self or individual goals, projects and interests, and does not imply nullifying consciousness, will and individual emotions.

The idea that solidarity means a personal sacrifice is originated precisely in those false conceptions of solidarity mentioned above, which conceive of solidarity as charity or welfare, or the obligation to pay taxes and pay more attention to subsidiary state activities. This is why we tend to associate solidarity with assuming behaviors and taking actions that benefit others by sacrificing something of ourselves.

But if we think of solidarity as sharing goals, then it does not mean denying ours to assume those of others, but rather to concatenate our objectives with those of others, involving a process in which our own goals are assumed by others, in the same way and to the same extent to which we assume theirs. Thus, what initially were our own goals expand and become integrated into a consciousness and a collective will that the group assumes. Therefore we enrich our own objectives instead of reducing them, proposing greater and higher goals, which are made possible precisely because they are not only 'my' individual goals, but 'our' shared goals, in whose accomplishment and achievement are all involved.

We will understand this better in the next chapter, when we examine the implications and impact of solidarity on each person, on groups and on the society.

VIII.

Solidarity is examined as a social energy that arises from the union of consciousness, volition and emotions: the 'C Factor'.

I now consider solidarity as an active force and as a constituent element of the new civilization, beyond what has already been discussed; a necessary condition that the initiators the new civilization must have.

Solidarity is a force, a powerful energy, apart from being a 'virtue' of people (although one of the meanings of virtue implies force). To be more precise and relate both notions, we will say that solidarity is a **value** found in inter-relationships and inter-subjective activities, which when lived and practiced specifically becomes a **virtue** in people which strengthens them.

In a theoretical presentation of a supportive or supportive economy, I formulated and developed the concept of a **'C**

Factor', which I identified precisely as **'solidarity turned into a productive force'**. Let us now extend this concept, which actually also applies to the new politics and the new culture (as we will discuss below, there must be a politics of solidarity and a culture of solidarity), and applies throughout all the process of creation of a new and superior civilization.

We call solidarity turned into a productive force the C Factor because it multiplies, because it acts efficiently producing significant effects. In economics, 'productive factors' is used to refer to 'productive forces' and 'productive resources". We represent solidarity with the letter C, because it is the first letter of many words which allow us to identify its real contents, such as community, cooperation, communion, common, communication, commensality, and all those words in which the prefix co- means "do something together".

But, what really identifies this C factor? How can we define it? **The C Factor is**, specifically, the fact that **the union of consciousness, volition and emotions of a group of people towards the achievement of certain goals or the performance of certain activities increases and multiplies the achievement of these objectives and the effectiveness of these activities**.

We say, 'union of minds, wills and emotions' for achieving certain goals.

The union of consciousness does not mean that everyone thinks alike, but rather consciously shared objectives, orientation in a common direction, to have achieved a significant level of communication between the members of the group, association or community of reference.

Union of wills means sharing purposes and really wanting to perform them, working to achieve common goals, deploying coordinated efforts to advance a process desired by the whole group.

Union of emotions means, for example, that all rejoice about something that benefits the group or any of its members, are saddened by negative situations, which cannot be overcome, that members encourage each other when faced with difficulties, and in general share feelings of affection between group participants and care for each other.

That the union of consciousness, wills and emotions multiplies results and achieves more shared goals in a group is a universal experience; a psychological, sociological and historical fact that has many manifestations and many examples. In a family united in purpose, whose members support and love each other, all are happier, children grow harmoniously and do better in school, parents have more success in their jobs, there is better integration into the community, and generally achieve the plans of the family better compared to other families in which disagreements abound. A soccer club in which the players are united, there is good integration with the trainers, there are good relations with club directors, and fans are firmly behind the team makes more goals, wins more games, obtains more triumphs.

There are numerous examples in history of smaller and more poorly armed armies but that were very united by their conviction of the cause for which they fought, which defeated more numerous and better equipped armies which were less cohesive and had little conviction or knowledge of the reasons for their struggle. In politics, cohesive parties and movements achieve better adhesion of voters and obtain better results than those in which there are factions and groups that divide it internally. The same is found in religious and cultural groups; the attraction of the faithful and the conviction of the faith of those who participate in them depend in very large measure on the community consciousness, will and the ties of affection that unite its members. Also in the economic area, companies whose workers, technicians, managers and owners are cohesive and feel a part of the company increase their productivity, which is much greater than in companies that have internal conflicts.

It is important to understand **how this community energy acts**, this strength of solidarity which makes it a multiplier of achievement.

A first way it acts is that the C Factor, as I have called it, **empowers each of the individuals** within the group. The power of belonging to an integrated group strengthens convictions, self-esteem and work capabilities. By contrast, those who are isolated or lonely are weaker and tend to believe themselves incapable of great achievements. When an individual poses objectives shared by others, and has a conscience, will and emotions which integrate her or him into a relevant group, they undoubtedly feel strong and capable of great things, because he or she knows, feels and verifies that others feel and act in the same way.

The second mode of action of the C Factor is to **enhance the group as such**, the collective, community or network. Since the coordination of actions becomes more fluid, the complementation of capacities allows things to be accomplished that otherwise would be impossible. We say that a united group integrates the strength of all its members and adds something more.

A third mode of action of the C Factor which makes the activity of all more efficient is that the union which takes place within the group, which is seen and appreciated by those in the vicinity of the group, **attracts the willingness of those around it**. The union of a group attracts others that appreciate this and want and aspire to belong to the same group. By contrast, observation of a group which has disagreements, fights and conflicts repels, drives away those who see it, because in general people do not want to be involved in the conflicts of others.

This is the way the C Factor acts; this is how solidarity becomes efficient and effective. There is more to say about this when the project is to initiate the creation of a superior civilization. I will examine this point in the next chapter.

IX.

A project as large as beginning the creation of a new civilization requires a very strong solidarity.

In order for solidarity to become a creative force, for the formation of a truly efficient and expansive C Factor, something more than friendship and companionship is needed; it is indispensable to have the practical cooperation of people who perform a common task. It also requires that people who share goals and who are bound by ties of affection propose higher goals which go beyond the interests and objectives of the group they form.

This is even more important when it comes to start creating a new civilization. To put it another way, there is collective selfishness to overcome. To create a new civilization we must create a C Factor: **a solidarity, welcoming and open to all**, **that is capable of spreading everywhere.** This is because a C Factor whose solidarity is closed corporately is not suitable for a project like this.

If we look at the great historical achievements, if we study the formation and gestation of civilizations, we find their origins in initially small groups of people, but empowered by two qualities that made them powerfully expansive.

The first is, precisely, that **their goal was a big goal, a great idea, a project which proposed to include the whole society, or that had the potential for genuine universality.**

Reaching a level of universal consciousness is more necessary than ever before in history, since the main problems that affect us, are problems that affect all humanity. The so-called globalization is highlighting this global dimension of problems, and that the possible solution is equally global. The issue of environmental and ecological imbalances teaches us that it is the earth as a whole which must enter into a new civilization. The globalization of information and communications enables us to be aware that we are part of a humanity that shares a common history and fate.

But the questions that arise and need to be answered are these: how can a universal consciousness be achieved? How can we universalize our own solidarity? These questions will be addressed later; for now I will affirm the following:

Access to a level of universal consciousness is not simply a matter of wanting, nor it is something you get by the simple desire to overcome selfishness. **Universal consciousness is constructed through the development of a project of universal dimensions. The understanding and drafting a project of a superior civilization is the real way to achieve a shift to a higher level of consciousness.**

I said that there are two qualities that have distinguished the small groups which have proven to be capable of initiating the creation of an entire civilization. The first is that of universality. The other, which I now consider, is that the C Factor they possessed was of immense power, a force in some ways overwhelming. Well, what is it that determines the power of a C Factor, of the efficient solidarity of a human group?

The answer is simple, and obviously consistent with the concept of the C Factor. The strength and energy which a group united by a consciousness, a will and shared emotions is capable of deploying depends on **the quality and intensity of the integration of their union.** It is thus essential to create a C Factor of the highest quality and greatest possible intensity. More specifically, the strength of the C Factor depends on the degree or level of union of conscience, willingness and feelings of the people who compose the solidarity group that shares a common goal. **The greater the intensity of unity and solidarity, the greater the energy generated in the group.**

This is a true "law" which acts even in the field of physical reality. The force fields that establish the union of physical or chemical elements are more or less intense, or attract and project greater or lesser intensity according to the cohesion or force that integrates the system. Nuclear reactions are more powerful than molecular and chemical reactions because the elements that make up an atom are much more strongly bound together than the components of a molecule or a chemical element.

The strength of the force that unites a group is more important than the size of the group or the number of its members. A tightly knit group of people is indestructible by normal means.

A solidarity group, although small in number, if held together by a consciousness, will and strong feelings can change the world. There are many examples in history. A small group of disciples of Jesus of Nazareth, who formed a community that shared everything, created a hugely expansive religion. A small group of faithful to Mohammad led a movement that came to be a great empire, whose decline was marked precisely by the breakdown of its internal unity. The great social revolutions, political and cultural, were started by small groups that began creating awareness, will and common sense, that bound very strongly.

Some people say, "a superior civilization is a utopia; a policy of solidarity, a solidarity economy are impossible projects". Maybe they say this because they do not know about the C Factor, or because they have not felt its power.

Once you form a cohesive solidarity group C Factor energy is generated, the members realize immediately that what previously seemed insurmountable difficulties now can be overcome, and they are capable of great achievements even though not having much money or power, or friends in high places and social contacts. Aristotle was the first to say that "great things can be done with small means and few resources", because he knew the forces that the human spirit can deploy.

I have said several times: union of minds, unity of will, unity of feeling. The three elements are equally necessary, because all three contribute to the cohesion of human groups and all three generate human and social energy. Some believe that solidarity is only a matter of feeling and emotions, others see it as something that depends only on conscience and ethical values, and others refer exclusively to praxis, to the will to achieve. What makes a human group indestructible, and certainly makes the initiatives they undertake viable and successful, is the integrity of their union. The three aspects contribute to the quality of the C Factor.

Everything depends, therefore, on the individuals and the group itself. In this way we will gradually clarify where to start. We already know that one of the first things that those who intend to start building a new civilization must do is to form around this goal a united group, one or more networks, one or more associations, one or more strongly united communities.

X.

Now the question of the size of the new civilization, which is not defined geographically. It is decentralized, currently local but tending to be universal.

I propose to turn now to a question which arises when it is proposed to begin building a new civilization. What might its dimensions be? And the related question, how will it expand?

As the answer I have to these questions is also considerably different from what is usually assumed when speaking of a historical civilization, it will useful to make some references to past civilizations.

There have been civilizations in history which were born itinerant and traveled and spread over large geographic areas, expanding their areas of influence and control around land and sea routes that they consolidated as they expanded. A case in point was the Christian civilization from its origins up to the consolidation of power of Constantine and the formation of the Byzantine Empire. Other civilizations have emerged installing their headquarters in a particular place (a sacred ceremonial space, a city, an island) which concentrated the activity of cultural creation and exercise of power, and from there radiated and grew to encompass a wide territory. An exemplary case of this kind is the Islamic civilization. Other civilizations have assumed defined territorial boundaries in the early stages of consolidation, so that their dimensions were defined by geographical boundaries which they protected and defended. This is the case of modern civilizations of states and nations. The various pre-Columbian civilizations in the Americas, as well as several civilizations that have occurred in Asia, also show a remarkable diversity in terms of their scales and modes of expansion.

Given the modern means of communication and transport, I think that today it is possible to establish and expand differently from all previous ways, making irrelevant the geographical dimensions of civilization; it does not even require a geographical or territorial basis. This implies that we must have another way to define who are its members and belong to it, and those who are strangers or foreigners.

And indeed, the new civilization that we visualize and whose birth we are observing is not itinerant, has no defined territory; it neither has nor requires a sole or main center of operations; it does not intend to establish itself in a particular geographical area. I say that the new civilization proposes to eliminate boundaries, decentralizing activities and initiatives, so that the areas of its presence become mobile, changing according to the places where there are people, groups and communities participating in it.

The new technologies and means of communication allow the internal links of the new civilization to be independent of specific locations, since its activities and initiatives can be coordinated and synchronized remotely.

Still, one must admit that everything always happens somewhere in space and at a certain time, so that there must be some things in specific locations; however, these will not be decisive or determinant.

The new civilization whose creation we are beginning already has and will have **multiple centers of initiative and operation**. It is being born and beginning to be established at each location where an individual reaches the level of autonomy and cultural, political and economic development that it demands, and in each area, locality or space where the process of self-organization and formation of networks that link, coordinate and enhance its development is produced. Each individual and/or group participates in the new civilization from wherever they are, from their own locality, and will extend their participation in it as the networks to articulate the cultural, economic and political activities that are part of the new civilization are extended.

Thus, being born and spreading every time a new member (an individual, a community, a network) is added, the new civilization will increase its numbers as its participants multiply, come closer to each other and become more interconnected.

If this is the way the new civilization is configured, we can say that it has a 'vocation to be universal ', since it may extended throughout the world, anywhere that creative, autonomous and solidary individuals and groups emerge that deploy the new economics, the new politics and the new culture that characterize it.

But along with affirming the "vocation" of universality, its tendency to be global, we must assume that, insofar as it is being created and established by the initiative of individuals and small groups dispersed in different latitudes and localities, the new civilization will have a distinctly local character, acquiring by what it does appropriate dimensions of economic, political and cultural self-organization.

The expansion of the new civilization from the local to the universal will be a gradual process of coordination among organizations, networks and locally based groups, which will be establishing among themselves diverse, multiple and increasingly strong links of communication, interchange and self-organization in the planes of their economic, political and cultural activities. **The new civilization is thus presented as a community of communities, as a network of networks, as an articulation and coordination between individuals and groups located in different places who share ways of being, feeling, thinking, relating and acting.**

If this is true, the task of each of the initiators of the new civilization has local dimensions: first to build the new civilization in themselves, and then build it in families, small local organizations, networks and communities, followed by extending it to other people, communities and groups that allow them to communicate, exchange, learn from each other and undertake joint activities.

Thus the task of building a new civilization that could have been imagined as titanic, acquires instead the proper dimensions of what appears to be perfectly attainable. It is a task, a creation and construction at the 'human scale'.

XI.

Explaining that the call of the new civilization is for everybody, and how individuals and groups can join it.

Related to the issue of the size and dimensions that the new civilization acquires, there is another important question that needs to be raised and addressed in a new way: Who are and who can we recognize as participants in the project of creating the new civilization? How do we recognize its members, and who gives them the 'badge' of members of the project? Which people and social groups can be and feel themselves part of the new civilization in the making? Is there perhaps a set of principles, definitions and beliefs to which one should subscribe in order to be recognized as part of the great civilization project?

The last question arises because we are accustomed to think in terms of the old politics, party and state, and the old organizations. All the questions are typical of those that arise and must be answered in advance by those seeking to organize, for example, a political party or a movement of social struggle or aspiring to obtain power. Even the movements that have emerged so far in order to build a new politics or a new economy have tended to do it this way; they established their headquarters, defined the mechanisms of integration and association, formulized the ideological manifesto, established the criteria and performance standards to be complied with by members, produced regulations and institutions that structured the movement, including how to elect leaders, to punish and exclude the maladjusted, etc.

Those who behave and think this way are still thinking in terms of the old civilization in crisis, and continue to organize and act according to the norms of this civilization, which require them to structure, guide, control and discipline their own forces. They do so because they still have not understood the nature and way of being of the new civilization.

The new and superior civilization we are creating convenes in a different way; it integrates and unifies in accordance with its superior modes of relating. First, **it calls everyone**, meaning it does not establish categories of potentially privileged participants (as would be convening workers, youth, women, intellectuals, adherents to a particular religion or belief, etc.).

The creation of a new civilization does not convene people to join a rigid, pre-established organization with an ideological project predefined by a particularly enlightened person or group, but **invites people to a participatory process of development, creation and searching for alternatives, to the definition and construction of a shared identity, to the articulation of a new project**.

But how can we produce, or expect to produce a definition of identity and shared project from so wide a social call with no predefined or explicit previous content? The reason is simply that in the course of a process of self-identification and self-organization as has been outlined, two complementary phenomena will occur naturally; on one hand the involvement and participation of individuals, groups, experiences and organizations, and on the other hand a process of self-exclusion. In other words, the self-integration or self-inclusion of those who are contributing to the culture and political and economic realities that constitute it, and self-exclusion of those who are not interested in these new realities or do not share these concepts.

Thus in the process of self-identification of citizens of the new civilization a dialectic between two elements will occur; on one hand the desire to belong and to participate in the common construction, and on the other hand the progressive intellectual and cultural definition, which in the process of being creating and reaching consensus among the participants will be defining its identity.

This is because a new and superior identity is both a factor of integration and exclusion; there are those who share the search, and those who follow other paths. But in this process there is no element of power and hierarchical authority; membership and identity will result from the independent decisions of self-inclusion and self-exclusion made by people, organizations, networks and communities.

Thus, although the invitation to participate is open to all, the demands of this integration (creativity, autonomy, solidarity) determine that those who respond to the call **will be only those really interested in a great project of civilization and the creation of economic, social, cultural and political alternatives.**

The powerful, the corrupt, those who are happy the current system, those who think that their needs are adequately met and their aspirations fulfilled in the framework of established society, those who prefer dependency to freedom, will not accept integration into the project to create the new civilization. And all who come once, if only out of curiosity, if they decide to accept this call, will remain in the process of identity construction and the large common project; that is, those willing to do their part, to participate actively, to think and discuss with others, to construct a collective creation.

You are part of the new civilization and share its values, benefits, environments and instances, to the extent that you help to create them. This is different from what happened in previous civilizations, which were joined as they were imposed by force or when they were adopted due to passive conformity or adherence.

The citizens and groups, networks and communities of the new civilization easily learn to recognize each other. It is not necessary to show a passport, as they are **recognized by the way they relate when they meet, in the manner in which they communicate, and also the contents of their communication.** These contents are not the typical, increasingly empty, poor and alarmed conversations that the inhabitants of modern civilization in crisis exchange among themselves (platitudes on the economy, politics, entertainment, daily life, and so on which have been transmitted previously by the mass media and State institutions), but rather the results of their creativity, their searches, their ideas, their work, their projects, their learning, their educational, economic and political initiatives.

How does mutual recognition happen among the participants? How is the identity of the new civilization defined? This is very interesting, and will be examined in the next section.

XII.

How do the inhabitants of the new civilization recognize each other, and how do they define the contents of their identity and project?

Mutual recognition and the process of developing their intellectual and moral content among the creators of the new civilization form part of the same dynamic expansion.

This starts from an initial situation in which the contents of the new civilization are not predefined, and therefore the project calls for virtually all people, initiatives, experiences and social organizations; however, not all feel called, only those who are willing to include themselves in it and participate in the process of definition. The beginning of the definition process is, then, self-recognition as part of the project, which is performed by each of the subjects who is motivated to participate. This self-recognition must seek and obtain the recognition of the other participants; thus the universe of the new civilization will be built up through the mutual recognition among its members.

This means in effect that each person, group, entity or organization that intends to participate in the new civilization must explain to others why they self-identify with it, which implies making explicit and precise, first to themselves and then to others that feel equally called, what are their reasons, motives, qualities, their merits to recognize themselves as participants in the new civilization and to aspire to the recognition of others involved in the project.

For example, persons, companies, organizations, universities, etc. that feel they should be among the creators of the new civilization will have to explain why they think they belong to and identify with it, expounding the ideas, initiatives and projects they have and in which they are participating, and their ways of being in these aspects, and why they define themselves as and wish to be recognized by others as part of the grand project.

Along with specifying the social subjects that integrate the new civilization, the ideals, the projective contents and values that define their identity will be determined, which will be the content provided by each member of the project.

Thus the new civilization will be defined and constructed not authoritatively, not academically, not following someone who preaches an *a priori* truth "that the new civilization is this or that, that it is here or there, that in order to participate in one must fulfill such and such specific requirements"; the process will be participatory, from the bottom, horizontal; it will be a process of self-consciousness and reciprocal recognition and convergence towards an identity that is built by all.

However, the rate and expansion rate of the new civilization will depend on the intensity and depth that the process of its real constitution acquires, which depends exclusively on its participants and the value of their ideas, feelings, creations,

works, relationships and experiences. If these are true, beautiful, attractive, persuasive and motivating, the new civilization will be true, beautiful, attractive, persuasive and motivating, and will increasingly attract more subjects and organizations who will be invited to participate and to merit self-recognition and be recognized as participants in its constantly renewing formation and identity.

To do this, it is necessary to advance simultaneously in the **creation** of the new, autonomous, superior project and culture that is capable of constructing the new civilization along with its **diffusion**, so that it will bring together creative thinking and articulate the desires of many who want to participate in the project.

Something should be said now about the 'diffusion', an issue that will be treated in depth later. Let's begin with an idea of Antonio Gramsci, who considered magazines and journals as particularly important. He hoped for a new type of magazine, which he conceived as **creative and organizer of a new culture**. In his time journals were the principal means by which the ideas and works produced by creators were disseminated. Today we have many new media for communication and diffusion. But the point is that he imagined **a rich and complex intellectual and publishing activity which unified creative activity with its communication**. He argued that the magazines should be interactive, to use the modern term, able to involve readers in the production of knowledge and new arts that are carried out more systematically by the creators and organizers of the cultural project. He said further that magazines must be accessible to different levels of readers, in addition to "meeting broad cultural needs."

But the most important idea is that creation and dissemination would be united in these journals, and that creators and readers would interact in the process of creation and dissemination. He also imagined many journals, at different levels, interacting and complementing each other in the process of creating the new culture. Later I will indicate why creation and dissemination must be part of the same dynamics, and why they should be interactive in both directions.

Gramsci conceived and imagined this great task of creation and dissemination of culture while he was in prison, but obviously he could not do it. The important thing for us is that he came to understand and conceive formally what is needed to start building a new civilization. He also probably understood that this was not feasible at the time, because magazines, publishing houses and journalism had technical constraints that made it almost impossible to do what he understood to be something formally required.

Gramsci could not imagine that the Internet and new communication technologies would greatly facilitate all this; but we know now, because we are experiencing it on our sites, blogs, portals, networks and diverse cultural portals.

Another advantage that we have now, which confirms that the time for the creation of the new civilization has arrived, is the fact that only now is it possible for creation and communication to be shared simultaneously and interactively. Before the creation of today's media, the Internet and networks, the creator or author of a work had to finish it completely before sending it to a publisher, who after evaluating it would decide whether or not to publish it and offer it to the public. Ideas and creations took a long time to diffuse and to reach people who would be interested in and motivated by them, who had virtually no way to interact with the author, and could do very little to disseminate and communicate to others what they appreciated. It also happened that many works were not published and distributed since they were not liked by the publishers, or whose content seemed to them too new and risky.

All this has changed completely, thus we are now able to advance rapidly in the creation and dissemination of the intellectual and cultural content of the new civilization.

XIII.

Here is presented the third quality that distinguishes the 'human type' of the new civilization: creativity.

I have stated that the initiators of a new civilization are creative, autonomous and solidary. Of these three qualities we have examined so far autonomy and solidarity. Now it is time to discuss creativity.

Clearly, creativity is essential to **create** a new civilization, which means, among other things, to find and develop new responses to problems that affect us and affect the world, and in particular to create a new culture, create a new economy, create a new politics.

However, the meaning of the creativity required must be defined. Creativity is a skill that all people have to some degree at least potentially, although some have developed it more and others to a lesser extent. Creativity is manifested, for example, in formulating ideas and projects, in suggesting solutions and original proposals for specific problems, in producing innovations in certain processes or structures that previously were conducted in conventional ways, and so on. Creativity is manifested in all kinds of human activities; work, study, science, art, technology, production, recreation, entertainment, etc.

The important thing is to understand that creativity can be developed and perfected by every person and by every human group. Developing it and perfecting it in individuals and in communities, organizations and networks, is part of the process of creating the new civilization, which its initiators will have to deploy. However, the development or atrophy of creativity depends on many factors, among which education, the type of teaching and learning and the way these are carried out are especially important.

And in this respect, creativity in the modern civilization in crisis is seriously deficient, which leads us to question the ways in which schooling and the education system are organized. Twelve to fifteen years of passive learning sitting hour after hour in front of teachers who pass on knowledge that students must memorize and repeat, have stunted the creativity of the majority.

In its beginnings and during its stage of development and consolidation, modern civilization needed and encouraged creativity, at least for the part of society and for the people who were expected to occupy leadership positions; these were the individuals who had access to freedom of thought, association and economic initiative. But for the majority, in politics for those who were led, in the economic area to employees and consumers, and in the cultural field for all those in which they wanted to instill new ideas, what was desired was a passive attitude of learning, obedience, submission, acceptance and conformity.

Thus the organization of education in this civilization is and has always been twofold; on one hand the education of the elite, and on the other education of the masses. The training and educational system is very different for the leaders and the led.

Currently, in the context of the crisis of modern civilization, much is said about innovation and creativity, but this is conceived as the search for greater efficiency and economic competitiveness, and does not contemplate the generation of new political ideas, new economic concepts or new sciences.

The creation of a new civilization is based on the expansion of creativity, as well as autonomy and solidarity. But as we saw that not just any autonomy or any solidarity is needed, the creativity of the initiators of a new civilization must also be special, since we are trying to create a new way of life, a new economy, a new politics and a new culture. What is needed is what we might call an eminent creativity. It is a type of creativity that has at its base, as a condition of its deployment, an opening, a free spirit and a willingness to think everything through again, to find new answers to fundamental questions, since what is required is to reinvent themselves and to invent, experiment and develop new ways to live, relate and act.

The creation and expansion of a new civilization involves, for all participants, a great development of creative capacity. This requires a radical change in pedagogy and ways of teaching and learning at all levels, from kindergarten to higher and continuous education. Of course it is necessary to learn the skills and knowledge already acquired by mankind and to acquire a certain knowledge base that is common to all people. But this "knowledge of the known" can be taught creatively, and not be just an assimilation and repetition of what others have done before.

Antonio Gramsci proposed an educational model that may be useful to develop a new educational system for the new civilization. He indicated three levels or phases of training.

The first phase he called '**active formation**' for the ages in which children are currently in elementary or basic education, which should **introduce children to the social and natural orders through activities of observation and experimentation which must accompany conceptual learning**. He emphasized the importance of training in the concept of balance between the social and natural orders, which is not a given balance but has to be built on work and the theoretical and practical activity of men. This phase should produce an understanding the movement and its future, and an understanding of the efforts and sacrifices of the past to produce the present, which will be needed in the present to produce the future.

The second phase or secondary education must be a '**creative**' **formation**. Gramsci suggested that the study and learning of creative methods in science and in life must begin at this stage, and not continue to be the monopoly of the University, or be left to chance in everyday life; this phase of training should already be helping to develop the element of autonomous responsibility and be a creative education of individuals. Creative education is the crowning glory of active education. **In the creative phase, building on the foundation achieved in the active phase, it seeks to expand the personality, which is becoming autonomous and responsible, but with a strong moral and social conscience. This means to learn by creating, and to develop the method of inquiry.** Gramsci wrote: "Discovering truth by oneself is creation, even if the truth is already known, and shows that the method is understood; it certainly indicates that the person has entered the stage of intellectual maturity in which new truths can be discovered. So at this stage, the main activity will be developed in seminars, libraries and experimental laboratories."

The final stage is higher and continuous education, in **which creativity flowers in the interplay between theory and practice.** Gramsci said that universities and schools should be reorganized and enlivened from top to bottom, providing students with specialized institutes in the various branches of research and scientific work in which they may collaborate and find the necessary subsidies for each form of cultural and work activity that they seek to undertake. They will need to establish permanent partnerships between intellectual work and external professional work.

This issue of creativity is a wide term that transcends education, and covers the development and dissemination of knowledge in all its aspects and dimensions. We will examine this point in more depth.

XIV.

We begin to examine the role of knowledge in the creation of a new civilization.

The development and communication of knowledge has a central and decisive place in creating a new civilization. In fact, **all civilizations have been preceded by the emergence of certain new cognitive forms, which opened the consciousness of people to the knowledge of previously unknown dimensions of reality, and that directed them towards new realities which could be created and elucidated.**

Human experience and consciousness expand, they open to new horizons, with the emergence of new structures of knowledge and its projection which precede them, and then govern them in the development of a new civilization. We can say that each civilization develops and has its own structure of knowledge and its projection; which we may call its own epistemological paradigm.

Karl Marx, who defined his philosophy as 'dialectical materialism', maintained that a new social formation could not arise until all the productive forces that would fit within it were developed, based on their specific social relations of production, and that new and higher relations of production never appear before the **material conditions** for their existence have matured within the old society. And he said that for this reason humanity proposes only the objectives it can reach, since these new goals arise only when the material conditions for their fulfillment already exist, or at least are taking shape.

This statement of Marx - which has given many problems to Marxists because it conflicts with the idea that a social revolution can take place without having to wait for the capitalist mode to exhaust its capacity of productive expansion – allows me to suggest (independent of materialism), that in fact what is required for the emergence of a new civilization is that the forms of knowledge and projection of the previous civilization have exhausted their capacity to understand and to project effective solutions to problems that emerge in their own crisis, and therefore within the old civilization there begin to take shape those new forms of knowledge structures capable of understanding, making sense of and projecting human experience towards the horizons of a superior civilization. I will argue that more than 'material conditions', what is indispensable are intellectual and cultural conditions which enable humanity to propose for itself these great new objectives.

It is often said that we are experiencing a transition to the 'knowledge society', and I think that what is happening at the level of knowledge is really part of a process to create the conditions for transition to a new and superior

civilization. What is most often said in connection with the 'knowledge society' is that the value and productivity of individuals, companies, workers, societies, is given more and more by their ability to learn, create and develop knowledge, disseminate and distribute it, and apply that knowledge to solving real and present problems, innovating, improving and transforming activities, processes, structures and systems. I think that the change which is currently involving the development of knowledge, its new structures and unprecedented forms of dissemination, is much deeper and more important than all this.

It is true that learning, development and dissemination of knowledge produces increased productivity and efficiency in any person or any company. But beyond that, **what knowledge produces, especially the new forms and structures of knowledge about which I will have more say later, is to enhance creativity, autonomy and solidarity of people and human communities in all aspects and in all their activities.**

New forms of knowledge and its projection that are developed in the process of creating a new civilization expand the consciousness of people, make them grow, improve, make them 'be' and 'be worth' more, in different areas of human activity. That knowledge, by growing and being disseminated in a community, an organization, a social movement or a network empowers them, makes them more creative, more autonomous, more solidary.

Because of all this, in those initiatives and activities which will start a new civilization, in the process of creating a new economics, a new politics and a new culture, a **decisive factor** in the outcome and progress that is obtained will be the capacity and application demonstrated by the people participating in these projects, in activities and processes to learn, develop, disseminate and distribute knowledge, and specifically the new forms and structures of knowledge of these activities.

Thus for example, the expansion and development of a new economy will depend mainly on the relevant knowledge which those interested and involved in its development learn, disseminate and apply. The viability of a political project of historical transformation will be proportional to the level and quality of knowledge its participants develop in its fulfillment. I even dare to postulate that the economics, politics and the civilization of the future will be built largely and primarily **from knowledge.** Consequently, the economics, politics and culture in the new civilization will take – will be able to take - different forms and contents according to the forms and contents of the knowledge that will be elucidated, and of the ways that their production and dissemination take.

Indeed, knowledge has always been fundamental in human history; but the impact of knowledge and its forms on the ways of organizing and carrying out economics, politics and culture is increasing dramatically, because now there is no human activity that is not subject to an enormous amount and variety of knowledge that imposes conditions on it, and without which it cannot be successful. We can say that, as never before in history, the development of knowledge is a necessity, and that upon it depends not only progress but the very survival of society.

But most the important idea I want to emphasize is that the transition from one civilization to another has always been preceded and governed by the emergence of new ways of knowing and projecting. The transition from medieval civilization to modern civilization was preceded and guided by the emergence of those new forms of knowledge - empiricism, positivism, the social sciences, the exact and natural sciences - which came to replace the religious, ethical and philosophical knowledge that prevailed in medieval civilization. In particular, knowledge of the positivistic sciences, interested in unraveling the 'how' of empirical phenomena to use them as instruments to favor production, led to the impressive industrial and technological development which today characterizes all economy and social life.

But, what exactly is this new form, and what are these new structures of knowledge that open us to a new civilization? What is, in this sense, the real novelty of the situation? I will reflect on this in the next chapter.

XV.

On the subjects of the new structure of knowledge and the role of the Internet and new communication technologies.

To begin the subject of the knowledge structures of a superior civilization, I will start by referring to those who are the subjects of knowledge, its creators and broadcasters, and related to this, the roles that Internet and new communication and information technologies are beginning to fulfill.

In medieval civilization and other past civilizations, the knowledge that provided the certainties that individuals needed to guide them in life and that societies needed to develop economic activities and establish social order consisted of religious beliefs, ethical norms and by the particular skills of each profession or work activity. These religious beliefs, ethical and practical knowledge standards were presented to all as 'given', even as sacred, in any case as indisputable. Such knowledge was transmitted from priests to the faithful, from father to son and from master to apprentice, and constituted knowledge accepted by faith, tradition and custom.

The sources of knowledge were encrypted, or written and disseminated in a language known as 'cultured' (Latin in the case of Western Europe), so that only a few initiates had access to them and could generate and disseminate knowledge. Even the practical knowledge of the trades themselves was kept secret by small organized guilds which defended their monopoly of these competencies. The relationship between the 'cultured' and the 'simple', between leaders and led, between priests and the faithful, between teachers and learners, was established by bonds of authority and obedience.

These forms of knowledge entered into crisis when knowledge began to be spread by publications in local or 'vulgar' languages. This secularized different aspects of knowledge, until Descartes put an end to these modes of knowledge with his famous 'methodical doubt', under which no knowledge acquired by tradition could be treated as sure. Empiricists and positivism soon established the emerging knowledge bases, when they affirmed that the only authority that could be accepted in knowledge was empirical information about 'objective' realities that each individual could verify with his or her own senses and experience. Thus the modern civilization of the positive sciences, industry and state appeared and became established. Industry and State in their modern forms were the result of the application of new forms of knowledge to economics, production, politics and social order.

Along with these, the number of people who produce knowledge multiplied. Scientists, intellectuals and ideologues were put into service of industry and the State, and knowledge and information developed as instrumental knowledge, as useful tools to establish and increase the economy and political life.

However, science and knowledge did not become popularized, but have remained as the patrimony of specialists, who maintain a monopoly on their knowledge by a double 'operation'. On one hand they have created a specialized and obscure language in which those who have dominated it through university education communicate with each other. On the other hand although there are efforts to 'divulge' science and knowledge, in a move to 'go to the people', only simplified and partly distorted results are transmitted, dogmatizing contents which are known to be precarious and subject to discussion and without disclosing either the methods or the arguments on which this knowledge is based.

In this modern civilization of State and industry, knowledge is institutionalized and professionalized, acquiring disciplinary and bureaucratic features that characterize the entire civilization. The university became the instrument for the formation of specialized professionals as required by the industrialist and statist civilization. This is knowledge put into the service of industry in all its branches, and the State in its various problematic functions.

In this context, the relations between rulers and ruled are based on a combination of technical competence criteria and bureaucratic control, by which are distinguished those competent to decide and control processes, and the subordinates who implement the decisions and comply with instructions they receive.

What is beginning to emerge now is something completely new and different. The media, the Internet and the social networks are completely changing the relationship of individuals to information and knowledge. There are three developments and transformations which are most significant.

The first is that virtually all individuals now have access to all kinds of information, ideas and knowledge from anywhere in the world. This is a change of enormous importance. Indeed, until recently people not trained in specialized disciplines acquired their pool of knowledge from what was transmitted to them by their family, school, state, political parties, churches and mass media. The information and knowledge received were organized, structured and programmed by the issuers. Now, however, everyone is the receiver and the public of every matter, of all the talk on all issuers, with the possibility and even the need to select for yourself what you receive and assimilate.

Thus the areas of freedom of each person have greatly expanded, and simultaneously the power previously wielded over consciences, over ideas and ways of thinking and feeling of the crowds by the few subjects who decided what should be known and learned has weakened. This facilitates the **autonomy** of individuals

The second important development is that each individual becomes a potential transmitter of information and knowledge. All persons who previously were only the public, passive recipients of information and knowledge developed by others are now able to be producers and transmitters of information, creators of new knowledge, which can easily put into circulation. This favors the **creativity** of people.

The third innovation introduced by the new information technologies is the establishment of communication networks, freely constructed by individuals, and with almost complete freedom of both input and output. What is involved in the formation of social networks is a fact of utmost importance that is going to modify and restructure completely the social organization and relations between individuals and between groups. It is the fact that everyone is able to pick and choose with whom they relate and to which groups and communities they belong. Things are changing from a situation in which the scope of social relationships was determined by the family and where one was born and raised, by the relations given by the neighborhood, school, church and work, to a new situation where everyone can freely choose with whom they connect and communicate, to what groups, organizations and communities they belong, in which cultural initiatives, social, political and economic activities they participate. This is again a huge expansion of the spaces of personal freedom, which in turn leads to the possibility of new and broader forms of **solidarity**.

In summary, we can say that with this transition to new forms of knowledge we have the opportunity to be more creative, autonomous and supportive. We may self-determine in our conscience and our social relations and develop our own social, economic, political and cultural initiatives, and need not limit ourselves to choose to participate or not participate in existing ones.

Society and history - the new civilization - can be built by individuals and by the networks and communities that we are freely forming, with the intellectual and moral content that we place in such initiatives.

XVI.

The participation of all people, and the role of specialists, intellectuals and scientists in the development of new science.

Now I ask a very interesting question; still dealing with the role to be fulfilled by knowledge and science in the creation of a new civilization. How can we solve the apparent contradiction between, on one hand, the claim that we are all elaborators of knowledge and active creators of the new culture, and on the other hand, the affirmation that a new and higher civilization requires a more advanced culture superior to that which has developed in modern civilization, and sciences that exceed the deepest knowledge and the finest developments so far achieved by the humanities and social sciences? Are we perhaps all philosophers and scientists, and all of the highest level?

Addressing these questions will lead us to understand and fathom one of the most interesting and conspicuous aspects of the new structure of knowledge that the new civilization will have.

In it, we are all producers of knowledge, based on our personal and group experiences. We are all formulators of questions, answer seekers, analysts of reality, thinkers. In fact, to some extent humans have always been all this; there is still nothing new yet. What is new is that these cognitive activities of each individual are recognized as valuable input, as valid contributions to be collected and integrated into a superior science and culture.

Antonio Gramsci, of whom I already said I consider to be a precursor and in some aspects the founder of a science of history and politics which aims precisely to contribute to building a superior civilization, suggested this question. He said that the new scientific understanding of the historical-political processes does not begin with some general conception of the world and history, but from experience. The opposite, that is, starting from a given philosophy would necessarily produce a subordination to some previous design, which would prevent the achievement of autonomy of the new science. But what would be this 'experience' on which the new science is based? It is certainly not the empirical data as understood by sociology and other social sciences, since these data are already processed orderings of reality based on determined theoretical conceptions, explicit or implicit, often structured according to the objectives and interests of leaders and dominant persons.

By **experience** Gramsci means specific historical processes, "history itself in its infinite variety and multiplicity"; experience that is lived by many individuals and groups, and configures what he called a 'living philology'. It is not data from sociological research, but a lived experience, composed of real actions and processes, of which the actors become aware. Thus Gramsci simultaneously opposes both a foundation of a speculative nature and a foundation of empiricist character of scientific knowledge.

This multifaceted experience dispersed among many individuals and groups needs to be articulated, put into relations, interconnected, in order to configure an integrated reality, to provide the process with meaning. This is verified first by the interpersonal communication of experiences that everyone has lived and experimented. Communicating individual experiences produces a progressive integration, coming to form a kind of collective experience in which everyone can feel a part of the experience of others. It is a process of reciprocal communication and learning in which the experiences, lessons and knowledge of many are shared.

This is where some special people must participate, actively analyzing and systematizing the experiences shared by many. We may call this the performance of a specialized cognitive function. This is a function that is assumed spontaneously by individuals who have become especially aware of the value of the experiences they have and propose to describe, conceptually organize and communicate them to others so that they will be appreciated and valued by many.

Between such 'systematists' and communicators there will also be established special avenues of communication, through media that they themselves create such as magazines, newspapers, radio, websites, blogs, networks, etc. The 'living philology' in this mode is configured as a large amount of shared knowledge already considered and systematized by a growing number of intellectually active and interconnected people.

This will make possible the emergence of who we can call great intellectuals, thinkers, scientists, creators of the new sciences. They will collect the experiences of all, reflect on them and go deeper, discovering connections between them, their dynamics and trends, bring to light their implicit rationalities, the logic of the processes in which the experiences of many are part.

This is the way that the new sciences will arise, which along with integrating the experiences and knowledge of many, having unveiled the previously hidden rationalities in the processes, can also make predictions, anticipating the future, projecting new dynamics that make more coherent and powerful the practical experiences that are taking place.

Later I will examine the conditions that make possible the emergence of a new science and in particular of those sciences which can understand, design and start building a new civilization.

Remaining for now with the initial question, that is, the need to express clearly the claim that all individuals are potential creators of knowledge based on their particular experiences and are independent seekers of truth; and the claim that a new civilization requires sciences which are comprehensive, autonomous and of the highest level achieved so far by human thought; it raises the question of how the creators of these sciences, the intellectuals and scientists who develop them can propose their scientific formulations as true sciences that deserve to be qualified as such, and show that they are providing necessary and universally acceptable knowledge.

Because, in the context of the creation of a new civilization, intellectuals and non- intellectuals, scientists and people who perform other functions in the economy, politics and culture, are all put on equal terms. There is no obligation or requirement that what one says must be accepted and embraced by others. In the perspective of a superior civilization that is founded on the autonomy of individuals and their organizations, communities and networks, no one can tell another what to believe, or how to understand reality, or how to solve a given problem using an argument based on some intellectual authority. In this sense what I explained earlier about the process of recognition among the participants of this new civilization is valid. We said that people and groups can simply present their ideas, their choices, their behaviors, decisions, etc., so they may be freely recognized and learn from each other.

Because, in the same logic of the autonomy of all, these higher, more rigorous, deeper, more comprehensive sciences are simply presented, disclosed to others, explaining their intentions and their claim to be recognized as part the creation of the new superior civilization.

That is, its makers do what should be done according to the logic of the creation of the new civilization, without imposing, without seeking followers; they simply offer their works for what they are, including their aspirations to be known and recognized, and they will be only insofar as they are useful, as they help to know, understand and project better than previous sciences. Above all, they will be recognized and accepted to the extent that those individuals and groups who participated in the construction of the 'living philology' on which superior constructs are based, recognize themselves in these constructs, and feel and perceive that their experiences have been fully incorporated, or criticized with valid reasons.

In the new civilization, specialists in science and knowledge do not act authoritatively, as occurs by contrast in the institutionalized disciplines and positive sciences of the old civilization.

XVII.

What conditions it make possible to create new sciences of history, politics and economics able to guide the creation of a new civilization?

We have seen that a new science and a new structure of knowledge are needed to start creating a new civilization. The question I will address now is: what conditions today make possible the creation of these new sciences of history, politics and economics, and this new conception of knowledge capable of guiding the creation of a new and superior civilization?

Since the aim of this volume is to answer the question of how to start creating a new civilization, I have only briefly critiqued the existing civilization, whose crisis is increasingly evident. I assume that in general these criticisms have already been made. This is especially true for the economy; the critique of capitalism and industrialism, which are the economic pillars of modern civilization, has been made for a long time and has been widely disseminated.

Criticism of the parties and the State, which are the political pillars of modern civilization, has also been made intellectually and has spread widely, though less obvious to many, as it has not yet penetrated into the common knowledge of most people. The critique of the cultural and cognitive pillar of civilization is the most incipient and least developed; it has been focused on the critique of the ideology but has reached only the positivistic sciences; sociology, political science and administrative, legal science and economic theory. These sciences still have a lot of prestige. Therefore it is necessary to dwell on the criticism of these cognitive structures of modern civilization, which are currently experiencing a crisis as profound as that which affects the economy and politics. Indeed, they **have lost their ability to understand what is happening and to plan effective solutions to real and current problems.**

One of the elements of the disciplines we know as the 'social sciences' is the fact that, having been established following the model of the natural sciences (without being sciences like them), they formulate explanations of social phenomena and processes based on the formulation of supposedly objective laws that govern the dynamism of historical reality, analogous to the natural laws which allow us to understand and explain physical and chemical phenomena. The social sciences speak of the laws of history, the laws of economics, sociological laws, the laws of politics.

However, human history is not a natural process which develops according to objective laws, but is the result of human activity and the groups that they form. **Human history is the praxis of men, it is not given naturally but is constructed subjectively, meaning by subjectivity more or less conscious and voluntary active intervention.** How, then, could 'laws' of history, economics and politics be formulated which have some effective predictive power?

If history is experience and practice in economics, politics and culture, the ways in which the experiences and practices of individuals and groups develop are the key to explain how economics, politics and culture are conceived and carried out in the sciences that formulate their structures and processes. Human praxis in modern civilization is very different from the praxis that is taking shape in the process of creating a new and superior civilization.

In the current modern civilization, individuals and the masses of the population remain essentially passive, because they are subordinates and act according to the guidelines imposed by the few who establish structures and the course of events. History is made by the dominant groups, which are guided by their special interests and shape the structures and the economic, political and cultural processes.

Well, how did the concept of regularities and laws in historical development appear? The 'laws of history' emerge as abstract generalizations of the way economics, politics and culture occur in modern civilization. In this the vast majority of individuals interact in the area of private interests, in which there is not a coherent political and historical activity. The activities of individuals and the masses do not produce activity which creates history; their actions are repeated according to passively accepted guidelines. The abstract generalization of that experience is what leads to the proposition of statistical and trend laws that describe and supposedly explain historical developments.

Since historical facts are not consciously desired or pursued by individuals or people in general, history appears to these individuals and people not as the result of concrete human praxis, but rather as something external to them; thus it can be interpreted as the product of natural forces acting with a predetermined logic, that is it determines unique historical events as part of a predetermined system of relations whose parts are 'legally' connected. But in reality these are not 'natural' forces, they are the imposition of the forces of small dominant groups (in the economy, politics and culture).

This is why, in situations in which the masses of the population are essentially passive, the formation of trend laws (of economics, politics and culture) provides a particular image of the result that the interaction of the activities of people and groups would produce based on their interests and private plans. By contrast, when conscious creative, autonomous and supportive action brings people out of passivity, this utility of the laws disappears when individual and collective action is oriented in very different ways than the current trends. History begins to be created by many, freely and consciously, and their dynamics can no longer be construed 'naturalistically'.

This is what happens in the process of creating a new civilization, a new economy, a new politics and a new culture, by the creative, autonomous and solidary action of individuals and groups.

It is very important to understand this, in order to suggest that we may be the creators of a new civilization. Then let me express it more simply. What was verified in the economy, politics and culture of the civilization that is ending was not the manifestation of historical laws or objective rationality, but certain 'regularities' and statistical constants in the behavior of individuals and groups that, based on the large number of people who performed and reiterated them, resulted in statistically identifiable trends. These regularities and trends are what the social sciences and found and formulated as if they were economic, sociological, political 'laws'. And what sustains and establishes these regularities and statistical constants of the behavior of individuals and groups?

It is not difficult to understand that these are actually the conscious actions of the ruling classes and leaders who impose their own objectives and particular logic on the whole society, manipulating the work and behavior of the masses. It is these dominant rationalities which are imposed on society as a whole, hidden under the idea that there are natural laws of history and that there are universal rationalities inherent in economics, politics and culture. By formulating 'scientific laws' in ideological and 'scientific' areas the leading sectors of society are actually 'passing laws' that induce conformist behavior of the multitudes that remain intellectually, economically and politically passive.

But when that economy, politics and culture enters into crisis and people start to abandon the behavior expected by the ruling groups, those economic, politic and social sciences fail to explain and predict the course of events. And then**, what makes it possible to create new sciences -** developed from below, from the immediate experience of individuals and active groups that make up the 'living philology', not formulated as a natural process subject to laws, but rather able to recognize the social and human subjectivity in the economic, political and cultural processes -, **is the emergence of active and participatory, autonomous, creative and solidary individuals, of self-organized and self-orientating groups who change history, who alter the dominant tendency, who are no longer guided by the established powers, who initiate the creation of a new civilization.**

These experiences and this 'new kind of historical situation' are the only means that allow the emergence of new sciences. They are the creative experiences of the new economics, new politics and new culture, which are theorized and projected onto these new sciences.

These sciences express the new emerging rationalities, and articulate them with the past from which they come, with the analysis of crises and problems to which they respond and even integrate and subsume - in the new sciences – those aspects of the previous disciplines and knowledge which are still valuable in the present, and therefore should not be discarded but integrated critically into a superior and autonomous knowledge.

XVIII.

Which refers to the structure of knowledge that opens to a new civilization and compares it with the structure of the social sciences of modern civilization.

When we become aware that we ourselves make and guide history, and economics, politics and culture, - and we only realize this when we begin to create a new and superior civilization - when we know we are protagonists and autonomous actors in history, then we can understand that the science of that history, and the sciences of economics, politics and culture cannot be disciplines that conceive reality as natural processes and objectives independent of the consciousness, will, emotions, ethics and values of those who are the creators, protagonists and guides of this history, economics, politics and culture.

The supposed objectivity of the economic, social and political sciences was based on a positivist and naturalistic conception of human reality which fades, or rather, is abandoned, as we become aware that **such supposed objectivity was on the one**

hand a theoretical and philosophical error, and on the other hand, we may say, a trick of the dominant classes and leaders who controlled and consciously directed history, economics and politics, presenting them as historical 'needs', as objective processes, as 'rationalities' which were given as if they were independent of their own interests and objectives. For the dominated and the subordinate, since they passively experienced the historical, economic and political facts and did not and could not feel themselves to be participants in these processes, such objectivity seemed real, because they did not guide the processes with their conscience and will.

Marxism itself, critical of domination and proponent of revolutionary transformations, also falls into the mistake of assuming a naturalized history, subject to objective laws independent of the will of men. It falls into error because it does not overcome the theoretical horizon of materialistic positivism and naturalism. And it makes this mistake because it does not conceive of human individuals as makers of history, proposing instead that they should just join the forces which are still assumed as objective; midwives of history who would act according to these objective laws in this historical necessity. This is even included in the theory in the idea that freedom is only the consciousness of necessity; that is, acting according to an alleged objective dynamism inherent in history, independent of the consciousness, will and the decisions and options that individuals and groups may take.

But we the initiators of a new superior civilization, freed from subordination to the powers and institutions of the civilization in crisis, our autonomy achieved based on the idea that each person is self-guided and the creator of culture, economics and policy, are able to overcome the naturalism and positivism in knowledge. For the creators of culture, who build it

85

consciously and freely, the sciences and arts and culture all are no longer mere superstructures determined by supposedly objective and necessary structures which function according to inevitable laws.

Thus we abandon the idea of objective social sciences, since we discovered that **all historical and social reality is subjective reality; that is, developed, built, led and coordinated by individuals and groups. Individuals and groups create them and thus include, in the reality they build, their own subjectivity, their values, ethics, goals, ideals, and also their deceptions, their wickedness, their negative values. All this is part of reality and therefore must be understood by science and become part of the explanation of historical processes.**

Therefore, scientific prediction is no longer merely a prediction of what will happen if human behavior continues to be automatic and regular, guided by the objectives and the dominant rationality; that is, a simple projection of current trends. In the future, prediction will be the statement of the results expected and predicted to occur as a result of the action of all the builders of the new economic, political and cultural realities.

Summarizing, we conclude that the new structure of knowledge and the new sciences that are beginning to be the cultural and cognitive pillars of the new civilization have profound differences in the social, political and economic sciences compared to current modern society.

While modern social sciences were developed by a few 'scientists', the creative sciences of the new civilization are developed by all, participating in different ways and with levels of expertise, and all will validate the new knowledge which will be proposed.

While modern social sciences are institutionalized and bureaucratic sciences, whose knowledge accumulates by the mechanical application of formalized methods and techniques, the new sciences are living knowledge, which are developed and proceed by dialogue and interpersonal communication between all the active people who are creators of history and builders of the economy, politics and culture.

While modern social sciences processes 'data' and 'information' collected by technical procedures which guarantee that from their analyses they can extract the expected validation of the assumptions made based on the pre-formed theory itself, the new sciences proceed by means of the multifaceted experience configured as a 'living philology' in which everyone participates. While modern social science focuses on the **quantification** of reality, favoring measurable dimensions and those that can be processed mathematically and statistically, the new science centers on the **understanding** of reality and its processes, paying particular attention to the qualitative, and especially to historical novelties.

Modern social sciences looked in the past for the causes of the presence, while the new sciences explain events and processes by their participants, thus they explain the future by the present.

While modern social sciences try to hide the subjectivity of both the 'object' of study and the knowing subject, so it will not interfere in the dynamics of the unknown reality, the new sciences reveal their subjectivity, precisely with the intention of intervening in history, to build it consciously and freely.

While modern social sciences attempt to consider social facts as things, carefully separating judgments of facts from value judgments and ethical assessments, the new sciences incorporate values and ethics in knowledge, both because they recognize them as present and active in historical reality and with the intention of projecting new realities which are superior to those of the civilization in crisis.

While modern social sciences are based, as a result of the above, on the historical passivity of the masses, and serve to control the masses and processes so they do not deviate from the prevailing and dominant rationalities, the new sciences intend to activate everyone, in order to release the conscious and free energy of people and to strengthen the emerging rationalities which the creators of the new economy, politics and culture bring.

XIX.

Here we begin to think of the new politics: a new structure of the organizing action of the community and transformer of social life.

Let us now begin to reflect on the 'new politics', which should be superior to what we know now, so it can characterize the new civilization that we intend to create.

I have already referred to the crisis that the political pillar of modern civilization has been experiencing for a long time, a politics that has developed based on the organization of parties, which have a singular way of relating to what they call the social 'bases' and intervening in the dynamics of the State.

In order to understand the issue we will address, it is necessary to distance ourselves from both the concept and the practice of politics as we know, and start from a general concept of 'politics', conceived as **the structure of the organizing action of the social order which also makes historical processes dynamic.**

With this concept of 'politics', we will understand as **'new politics' a certain structure of the organizing action of the community and transformer of social life, and specifically the activity which, from the present reality, initiates the creation of a new social and institutional order proper to a new and superior civilization.**

We could also conceive the new politics as **the set of theoretical and practical activities that can solve the organic crisis of modern society by creating a new civilization.**

We begin with the assertion that the party form of politics has definitely entered into crisis, and this is a substantial part of the crisis of the organization of the state in modern civilization. If this is true, it is obvious that the historical overcoming of this crisis cannot be achieved through politics and parties as we have known them, it is necessary to develop and test a new set of transforming activities, able to start the transition to a new civilization. In other words, it is necessary to develop a new paradigm of politics.

When we speak of a 'new **paradigm** of politics', we refer to a **theoretical conception** of the transforming and organizing action of the social order; a theoretical concept as an expression of the rationality of the **practices** and transformative actions that begin to be manifested in the processes of creation of a superior civilization, and that are able to promote, enhance and take those processes and actions to levels of greater coherence and effectiveness.

I have called this new theoretical conception - using an expression of Antonio Gramsci - 'the science of history and politics'. Pasquale Misuraca and I, in the second volume of the book **"La Travesìa"**, said that this science "is not trying to develop a new science based on existing politics, or to deploy a new politics based on existing political science, but to build together a new cognitive structure and a new structure of the transforming action, in an original relationship between them".

I intend now and in the following chapters to present some elements that characterize this new structure of the transforming action, that have been appearing in the theoretical development as we analyze the practical experiences of an emerging 'new politics', and seem consistent to me with the proposed transition to a new civilization which we want to be creative, autonomous and solidary.

The first element of the new structure of the transforming action that clearly distinguishes it from the politics of modern civilization is that **the politics does not consider its objective to be the conquest of power and control of the State**; it does not even seek to accumulate political power to exercise over a class, groups of the masses or the whole of society.

On the contrary, **the new politics is geared towards the social spread of political power, that is, to empower individuals and communities and groups working from the civil society.**

It wants every person and every community, organization or social network to regain control of their decisions and their living conditions, implying also that they do not aspire to exercise power over other people and other groups, but that each person seeks to guide himself or herself and has as much power as needed to guide herself or himself consciously and freely.

The concept of empowering people and organizations of civil society, involving a process of social dissemination of power, is directly linked to the emerging **demand for participation** which appears in virtually all initiatives and searches oriented to achieving social changes**.** Creative, autonomous and solidary people want to participate as protagonists in organizations in which they form a part, and in the diverse instances of economic, social, political and cultural life, and in all places where important decisions are made that affect their lives. They want to overcome the feeling which is so common of being part of larger systems, structures and organizations in which they play a role or a function, but where they have influence on their objectives, their operations and their overall functioning.

But not all claims and forms of social participation are expressions of the new structure of the transforming action. For example, given the enormous concentration of power that in modern societies has become centralized in the State and its parties, and while the implications of assuming responsibility for one's own decisions are not yet completely understood, often the attempts at participation lead to inorganic mass actions, aimed at pressuring those holding political power, so that they will make the decisions and do what the pressure groups want to achieve. But this way of channeling social participation is part of current modern politics in crisis, and maintains the strict separation between those in power and those who can only protest and pressure. It is a form of social action that has occurred throughout the history of modern civilization, and has achieved very few results of effective transformation.

But it is not just because of the ineffectiveness of this form of political participation that it does not correspond to the new structure of transformative action. Faced with a power, creating a counter-power that confronts it is the style of politics characteristic of modern civilization, which makes power, that is concentrated heavily in the State, the key to the construction and maintenance of social order.

Creating social and political power opposed to the dominant power one cannot build a civilization of autonomous, solidary and creative people, communities, organizations and networks. This is because the exercise of power as occurs in modern politics implies relations with people and organizations in such a way that a few are able to make many others follow decisions emanating from the will of those in power. This is configured as a relationship of domination and subordination according to which some rule and others obey, some direct and others follow orders. It thus maintains a hierarchical, vertical situation that distinguishes and separates the members of society into leaders and led.

The growing awareness of this as a structural problem of modern politics leads us to change the perspective in which participation is sought; more than a way of fighting for access to the central power, it is an effort at **decentralizing and social dissemination of power**.

This is the direction we see in processes that focus on regionalization and the strengthening of the so-called "local powers", in which citizens find possibilities of direct participation; participation based on autonomy, which encourages creativity and creates bonds of solidarity.

We are so immersed in current modern civilization, so accustomed to its concepts and modes of relationship that it is hard for us to conceive of a different civilization in which the social order does not constitute a power base from which some people exercise over others. But the fact is that this mode of social organization is in crisis, and there are more and more people and groups who refuse to be led by others, since they want to direct themselves and aspire to control their own living conditions.

The reflection on the new structure of the action organizer and creator of a civilization is just beginning. I will expand it in the next chapter.

XX.

On the 'unifying form' of the new civilization, or how it creates unity and social integration around the project of its creation.

When we talk about empowering self-directed people and groups, of the social spread of power and decentralization of decision making - concepts of a new paradigm of politics- it is likely that many associate this with anarchy, and thus with disorder and chaos. Indeed, the absence of centralized power and groups of leaders who use a mix of domination and consensus to ensure social order could lead to a seriously disordered and chaotic situation, if it implied that every individual and every group were guided by and acted only according to their own interests and wishes. In other words, individuals configured in the manner of modern civilization, that is, individualistic and competitive, consumerist and educated for subordination, immersed in a capitalist economy and a highly concentrated market, in the absence of a State or a political order which organizes and disciplines them, would surely give rise to a state of affairs that would be very far from being a social order, and even further from generating a new and superior civilization.

The situation is different if there are independent, creative and supportive individuals and groups, in the sense that we have defined these three founding qualities of a new civilization. But also in this case, achieving social integration and a superior political order implies the deployment - as part of the new structure of the transforming action – of social processes which are organizing and integrative.

The new structure of transforming action must create and deploy its own ways of generating unity and social integration. We come thus to identify a second element of the new politics.

Indeed, every civilization requires something that unifies and integrates its components, that is, the individuals, communities, societies, countries, etc. that compose it. Studies of civilizations indicate that, together with a particular 'human type' that characterizes them, civilizations have always had a **'unifying form'**, which in past civilizations might have been an empire, a church or a religion, and that in modern civilization is the national States.

Up to now, the 'unifying form' of civilizations has been imposed on its members through a combination of two factors or integrating forces: on one hand force, that is the military or bureaucratic domination by those in power, and on the hand the consensus or acquiescence of subordinate members with respect to a certain worldview, philosophy, religious belief, political ideology or moral doctrine.

However, we have seen that in the project of a superior civilization based on creativity, autonomy and solidarity of its members, neither force and discipline imposed around a center of power, nor a predefined doctrine or ideology which generates only membership, consensus or conformity of those who are subordinated as 'led' to groups which proclaim themselves 'leaders', is adequate. **It is therefore necessary to build unity another way, and develop a different way of integrating the components around a new "unifying form."**

As a means of creating new cultural unity, Antonio Gramsci postulated the need for "a homogeneous cultural center" which, through a formative-educational-training, develops and promotes a collective consciousness using a determined historical-social base which contains the specific premises of this elaboration. He added that this center cannot limit itself to the mere theoretical statement of 'clear' principles, which would be an illuminist mistake, a pure action proper to 'philosophers' typical of the Seven Hundred. Building on this idea, Pasquale Misuraca and I postulated in the book *La Travesía*, "it is necessary to have a center for the production, management and dissemination of theoretical and practical activities which carry the new historical rationality, which act as a meeting point and synthesis of multifaceted initiatives and experiences; a center of coherent intervention for all the different activities, institutions, organizations, individuals and existing economic, social, political and cultural forces, to renew them from within and redirect them in a common perspective."

In fact, rather than <u>a</u> center of production and dissemination, which is needed are **multiple centers connected by a network and united with each other**, because this is what is required by the task of collecting and integrating so many diverse and dispersed experiences, ideas and initiatives, and for so many active participants scattered around the world to act together.

97

However, this is only a tool or a means of unification and integration. The important thing is for the unit to think and act creatively, guided by the central idea that **unification occurs in the convergence towards a common project, which is the creation of the new civilization.**

There must be convergence from diversity, approximation to a shared place from various starting points and following multiple paths. These paths start from different, unique situations, but lead to a meeting point, which is the draft of the new civilization. This project, as we have seen, gathers up the diversity of motivations, desires, experiences and perceptions which are being developed autonomously and supportively by the creators of the new civilization.

In this way will be recognized, in the unit that is being constructed, the infinite richness of diversity of those who bring their own ideas to the convergence, which will be recognized by others when they are elements that enrich the common project.

What makes the elaboration center or centers of development and dissemination unifying is a specifically intellectual task of comprehensive, integrative elaboration; and once this is done, to give to each participant and contributor the overall vision, in which the contributions of all are recognized, integrated and valued.

This center, or this network of centers of development and communication, is not established as a power which centralizes and disciplines bureaucratically or authoritatively; it is rather a center or a network of centers that build unity by the development of integrated and comprehensive syntheses of multiple preparations. These will be unifying centers that elaborate and disseminate, that collect and return.

This involves producing these elaborations and these syntheses in public, in front of everyone, showing the development of the syntheses as they are connected to the input received. The 'unifying form' of the new civilization is elaborated not by power, but by the same comprehensive elaboration of the plan to create the new civilization. **The 'unifying form' of the new civilization is, precisely, its project.** It is about creating a unifying non-bureaucratic form which does not unify by control and conformity, but rather by the cultural integration of many of those involved in the drafting of the New Civilization. It is the project that unifies.

In the construction of a common project, we all pursue and develop our autonomy and our creativity, and in doing so we become supportive, as I defined the concept earlier, which comes from solidarity and the Latin word 'solidus', and which we understand as a community or human collective group **unified** by fundamental ideas and truths, by shared values.

XXI.

About the primacy of civil society in the new policy which is not 'partisan' but inclusive of diversity.

We wonder now if there is any activity, or some dimension of social life, which we regard as central to the new structure of the transforming action, and which will therefore be determinant in the process of creating the new civilization.

In modern civilization it has been argued forcefully, by most intellectuals and organizations which have had the intention of transforming society that politics is of prime importance; it would be the central activity. That is why it has been argued that all societal change must begin with the State, which must first be 'conquered' by political subjects carrying the transformative project.

According to what has been argued above, the primary or central factor in the new civilization should not be in politics, but rather in culture and knowledge, which due to their ability to fix objectives of historical development and to give meaning to human life will be able to guide and direct - not authoritatively or bureaucratically - both social processes and economic and political processes. The economy and politics would be oriented in accordance with the human development objectives established in the field of culture and knowledge sharing.

This makes **civil society** the preferred place for the integrative and transformative action, that is, for the new politics, unlike what happens in current modern civilization in which policy is developed preferentially at the level of the political society and the State.

This statement, however, must be considered as temporary and vague, because the distinction between civil society and political society responds to a separation between two spheres; the public power on one hand, and private, community and non-government activities on the other, with the leaders at the top and those directed at the bottom. This separation that happens in modern civilization should not be reproduced in a new and superior civilization.

However, the assertion of the primacy of civil society makes sense now, as long as civil society and political society are separated. This is why, given that we must start with the current reality to transform it, the new politics begins to be constructed from existing civil society, and **through its own development and deployment the new politics is shaped within civil society. Thus once the new politics is constructed within the civil society** and once the future civilization is formed, the distinction between civil society and political society will no longer be a distinction between different realities, but merely an epistemological distinction. To state this more specifically, **in the new civilization there should not be a 'political class' separate and distinct from civil society**.

The transforming action is not concentrated in the State or government; the primacy of politics is not accepted; the transforming action is displaced from the political society to the civil society. The reason for this shift is that the new system of transformative action is aimed at overcoming the civilization of politics, political parties and the State, and at overcoming the distinction between rulers and ruled. If instead we define the transforming action in the context of political society, we would remain in the politics which are characteristic of the modern civilization and social order in crisis.

An obvious consequence of what we are saying is that in the new politics we are not trying to create one or more new political parties. The 'political party' entity is characteristic of modern civilization; the first historical instance was the Jacobin party, and its nature is incompatible with the new civilization we want to create.

There are several reasons for this incompatibility, but the main one is the fact that, by definition, a political party is the organization of a particular group, that by grouping separates itself from and tries to rise above the community with the intention of directing it. Armed with an ideology or doctrine and representing the interests of one sector of society, the party is created with the vocation of power, with the explicit or implicit intention of promoting its ideology or doctrine and its sectional interests, using for this the complete or partial control of the government of the State. And since there are several groups that aspire to the same thing, each aspiring to represent a part of society and promoting a particular ideology or doctrine, society tends to divide politically, or more precisely, to 'split'. Because of this, political parties fight each other, vying for the favor of the citizens and the power of the

State; consequently political parties generate division and conflict in society. There are parties that explicitly declare this way of being, and others which may deny it, but this is the way political parties are and act in today's society.

By their very nature political parties affirm and act the 'centrality of politics'. The centrality of the 'civil society' of which we speak involves a very different way of organizing social life and performing historical transformation. The centrality of the 'civil society' above all means that the new politics is built 'from below', from what is now subordinate, from what the parties often call the 'social base'. By overcoming this subordination, people and their communities, organizations and networks will deploy their own activities of regulating and social transformation. They are not doing it from power concentrations that have been elevated above the community and in which they do not participate. **In this sense, the political order is configured as a community of communities, as an organization of organizations, as a network of networks**.

Proceeding in this way, the 'civil society' will progressively become a 'political society'; a civil society will develop that is politically active, and a political society that will no longer be separated from civil society, since it is the civil society which configures and establishes the social order necessary for the development, transformation and improvement of human life.

The new politics is not 'partisan' but rather an integrator of diversity, and is not the expression of the peculiarities of human groups differentiated by their ideological and corporate interests, or social classes or groups. But then two questions arise: What does the new politics do with the different ideas and different points of view of people and social groups? And what does the new politics do with the different special interests of groups and social sectors?

I will address these questions in the next chapter.

XXII.

On how the new politics accesses to the universality using its different ideas and different interests.

Let us now examine an important issue that we raised at the end of the previous chapter, and on whose answer fundamental aspects of the new civilization depend.

Reflecting on the 'form' that could unify society in the new civilization, and affirming the centrality that the cultural and cognitive activities that are performed from civil society must occupy, I said that the new politics is not 'partisan' but rather an integrator of diversity; not - as in current policy- expression of the particularities of human groups in conflict based on their different ideological convictions and their corporate interests, or of their social classes or groups.

Now this conception of the new policy raises two crucial questions: What does the new policy do with the different ideas and different points of view of people and social groups? And what does it do with the different interests, groups and social classes or sectors?

I can give an initial response to these questions by saying that **the new politics makes a systematic effort to collect from every ideological, doctrinarian or theoretical viewpoint what it contains that is genuine and constructive, integrating the different approaches into a comprehensive view of them all**. **Similarly, the new politics aims to recognize what is fair, legitimate and relevant in the interests expressed by each group or social category, seeking to link them all in a perspective of common or universal good.**

But if this is the easy answer to the questions raised, the difficulty appears when we ask how this is done specifically, who can do it, and by what specific processes.

In this regard, the first thing I can say is that it is not through the composition of forces in the State -as supposedly occurs in the democracies of modern civilization- where the articulation of interests and ideologies will be found. Historical experience shows that in the modern state social and cultural integration is very precarious; usually in the State there is predominance of a particular group, party or alliance of parties and a particular ideology.

In the new politics, the process of cultural integration is offered to each person, because the new politics is always achieved starting from people, who as we have seen are the first subjects of the new civilization. The subject of political ideas and political interests is always first the person, and then the communities, organizations and networks that they create.

But the project of the new civilization implies access to an universal point of view. It is universal in the sense that it expresses a universal human consciousness, and the interest and the good of the whole society. It is not universal in the sense of a general and abstract concept that is expressed through 'principles' and values formulated abstractly to which everyone can say they ascribe but not really assume in what they imply, but rather in the form and with the content of a concept and a political project that can be assumed theoretically and practically by all people and all groups that constitute the new civilization.

The specific task of the new politics will thus be to move progressively from the individual position of each person and each group to a universal position. This involves a process of progressive expansion of the perspective that by stages overcomes personal and group boundaries, creating circuits that will become increasingly wider until they encompass the entire society, until they become universal.

The path from the particular to the universal is accomplished by each person, each group and each political subject. It implies an expansion of the consciousness of each subject, individual or group. And since the starting point is always and inevitably different, because it corresponds to the experience and ideas, goals and interests of each person and each particular group, there will be as many paths to the universal as there are individuals and groups conducting the search, the transition to the universal.

Now, it would be totally illusory to think that the process can be taken directly from the individual to the universal in one big leap. **Intermediate stages** are required in a construction process that ascends from individual people to the entire society, passing through local and regional instances, individual organizations and sector groups.

This assumes that individuals and groups will be relating, dialoguing and uniting solidarily, so that the process acquires greater and greater intersubjective dimensions, but more importantly increasingly rich content, as the experiences and learning of some are shared and enriched by the experiences and learning of others. Thus an integrative politics is formed which unifies society, really oriented to the general good of mankind.

It is important to make clear that access to a universal point of view both in the areas of ideas and interests by definition assumes the acceptance as our own of the intellectual paths and legitimate interests of individuals and groups with whom we communicate and interrelate. But this assimilation of what others suggest cannot be eclectic, as simple addition, since this would imply only dispersion and incoherence.

To 'accept as our own' the views of others involves integrating them into our own conceptual and practical experience. This can be accomplished only through a process of criticism, in the sense of submitting to our own analysis what is initially foreign, extracting from it only what can be coherently integrated with our own ideas. However, if we start with the necessity of universality, criticism cannot just deny the foreign, but must lead to its critical integration. Always and inevitably this will involve overcoming one´s former views, accessing a new and superior point of view, superior compared to both our previous ideas and those of the others.

Thus **autonomy is achieved in politics; it will be more autonomous to the exact extent that it is more universal**. For if our viewpoints do not widen and become more universal they will be absorbed by another, and it will be that other that will guide the political process. The greatest politicians will be those who are most advanced on this path of globalization, and they will be great and recognized as such by having proved themselves capable of assimilating and integrating a greater proportion of viewpoints, experiences and interests into a conception and a great coherent political project.

XXIII.

Reflection on the "adversaries" of the new politics and how to relate to those who challenge it.

Another question that arises when considering a new paradigm of politics refers to the opponents. Are there any opponents in the new structure of the transforming action? Who would they be, and how can adversaries be identified? What kind of relationships should be established with adversaries?

In the politics characteristic of modern civilization, for each political party and movement opponents have been clearly defined. The adversaries are established as such, often even as enemies, by every political subject, by each party. The opponents are the others, those who are different, those who think differently, the social groups to which we do not belong. Thus in modern civilization politics is struggle and confrontation between adversaries and the identification of adversaries is a fundamental and decisive question for each political party. Without adversaries it seems that there would be no politics, there would be no "cause" to fight for.

In fact, modern politics has many warlike characteristics as shown by many of its concepts, which have been borrowed from the military and war language. Words like militancy, conquest, strategy and tactics, trenches, winning or losing positions, strategy of movements, strategy of positions, maneuvers and alliances, advances and retreats, coordination of forces, are all words that come from military language, and are used abundantly in party politics.

When it comes to creating a new civilization, we can think of something like adversaries, but the word "adversary" takes on a completely different meaning than it has in modern politics. In a superior form of politics, opponents would be those elements, features or aspects of reality that we do not want to be present in the new civilization. For example, opponents would be hunger, injustice, crime, poverty, competitive individualism. Opponents would be the problems of society we want to overcome, transform and take to higher levels. The new politics has a critical and antagonistic dimension with respect to those aspects of reality we do not want to be present in the new civilization. But we will not think about people, communities, organizations or different groups as opponents to be conquered or subdued.

The relation that in the new politics should be established with people and groups that are antagonistic to the new civilization project and to the new politics should be first and foremost knowledge of their motives, and on that basis, the valuation of their potential. It is possible, indeed, it is sure that these individuals and groups who oppose us express certain demands, ideas and values that could be incorporated, although perhaps on a subordinate level, in the project. On this basis, it will be possible to establish a relationship with these supposed 'adversaries' aimed at creating in them particular development processes of transformation and improvement;

processes which they carry out themselves, although favored by our communication with them, and that lead them to join the new civilization.

Related to this, I cite a concept of Antonio Gramsci that I find very lucid. Gramsci says that "finding the real identity under apparent differentiation and contradiction, and finding substantial diversity in apparent identity is the most delicate, misunderstood, yet essential quality of the ideas of the critic and the chronicler of historical development." I think this intellectual quality also applies to the new politics.

If we define the new politics as an activity of social organization and as making change dynamic, **we must work with all people who form current society to develop them, make them dynamic and integrate all in the new civilization.** In a superior civilization as we conceive it there cannot be either excluded or subjected people.

That is why Gramsci argues that the 'unitary development center' of the new culture should keep track of **all** movements and intellectual centers that exist and are formed. Of all, excluding only those that are arbitrary and crazy; even these, with the strength they deserve, must be at least recorded. He added that it is necessary to 'draw' a kind of intellectual and moral **map**, that is, to identify the large movements of ideas and the great centers, taking into account the innovative **impulses** which they contain. He added that it is not necessary to wait for them to acquire their full force and consistency to pay attention to them, nor is it necessary that they have the qualities of consistency and intellectual wealth, because it is not always most coherent and intellectually richest movements which succeed.

The reason for this 'monitoring' is not just to have knowledge of the cultural reality, but mainly to organize our own dissemination of activities and to make the project of the new civilization universal, acting on these existing cultural movements, indicating to them what they must overcome, and helping them to develop best in what they can contribute, always seeking their integration into the new civilization. **In all cases the idea is to widen the field of possible consciousness by entering into communication and dialogue, thereby enriching and widening the project itself, progressively extending it to the necessary universality.**

Sometimes the criticism must be tough, even ruthless when necessary to overcome the lies and deceptions, domination and exploitation; but we must always leave room for the reception, integration and the recognition of that which is valuable in those who contradict us and in opposing groups.

I will continue reflecting on the 'new politics' in the next chapter.

XXIV.

On the transformative dimension of the new politics. How much continuity with the past and how much a new creation?

I have said that politics is **the organizer of social action, and also a revitalizing action of historical processes. Based on this general concept of politics, I affirm that the 'new politics' is a certain structure of this action of organization of the community and transformation of social life, that from the present reality starts creating a new social and institutional order worthy of a new and superior civilization**.

This raises a new crucial question: How much continuity with the past and how much transformative action? How much tradition and how much creation, how much should be conserved and how much should be changed in the new politics? More precisely, it is trying to conceive the relationships that may occur in the process of creating the new civilization between continuity and novelty, between tradition and the project, between conservation and change.

When I raised the issue of social and cultural integration and the 'unifying form' of the new civilization, I focused on the first dimension of politics, that is, in politics as an organizer of a new social order. However, in the transition to a new civilization, at the beginning of its creation, the transformative dimension acquires special importance and centrality.

In the modern politics which is already definitely in crisis, the transformative dimension of politics has been defined in two different ways and accordingly has produced two different models of politics: reformist and revolutionary politics.

Reformist politics emphasizes the continuity and preservation of the existing order, which is conceived as capable of being made more dynamic and partially modified, but in such a way that the existing order and its fundamental continuity are not affected. The intervention in the historical process is by means adaptive reforms which do not disturb the social order. Even more, the partial reforms are posed with the precise aim of anticipating possible threats to the established order, which runs the risk of disintegrating as a result of the conflicts which are produced and accumulated within it if it does not evolve.

It is quite obvious that this model of reformist politics is useless when it comes to start creating a new civilization, because it is consciously aimed at preserving the existing institutional, economic, political and cultural order and reducing change and novelty to secondary aspects, and including historical dynamics only in terms of improving already established modes of operation of economics, politics and culture.

The other model, **revolutionary politics** emphasizes transformation, so that the structures of the existing order are subverted and replaced by a radically different social order. Revolutionary politics supposes it to be possible to change an economic, political, social and cultural 'system' to an entirely different one, and this in a short period of time, through a process of structural transformation precisely called 'revolutionary'. The way to do this is the seizure of State power by the party or group with the revolutionary project, and then from the State imposing the new realities, the transformations, to the whole society.

This revolutionary political model is also incompatible with the creation of a superior civilization, because it involves a process of concentration of power that denies the essential values of civilization that we want, and involves an extreme enhancement of the State, that is, strengthening precisely the central unifying institution of the modern civilization in crisis.

Thus we see that **both the reformist model and the revolutionary model function to maintain the old current modern civilization**, although for different reasons and by different means.

The new politics, oriented towards a new historical civilization, requires a completely original combination of historical continuity and the creation of the new. On one hand we must recognize that the element of continuity is essential in the creation of a superior civilization, precisely because it is a civilizing process which proposes to lead to superior forms of human coexistence. The extreme break with the past typical of revolutionary movements usually generates dynamics that in many cases have been described even as barbarism, since they have emphasized the destruction of what exists more than overcoming it. It has also happened historically that a new civilization is inferior to the previous one, and this happens precisely when the elements of destruction and discontinuity with the past are taken to the extreme.

A movement to create a new and higher civilization is inserted in the dynamics of what may be the process of maximum historical length, the process of civilization of mankind.

The political movement aimed at creating a new civilization requires an awareness of its own duration and its place in history, consciously being a process that is rooted in history but projects towards the future, in the process recovering everything valuable, positive and redeeming that mankind has created over the past centuries and millennia in the fields of economics, politics, culture, the arts, thought, spirituality, etc.

The creators of a new and superior civilization must develop something that could be called a 'civilizing spirit', i.e. having a "sense of civilization", which is a kind of historical consciousness, the 'long term' of the evolution of humanity. This 'spirit or sense of civilization' implies assuming that the movement itself is a moment in a long and complex process which is very old, has been going on for centuries and millennia, and continues and is projected into the future. **This awareness of history is, in short, a real and concrete manifestation of the establishment of a relationship of solidarity with all humanity.**

But of course not all of the past should be kept. What deserves to be preserved is that which the past has that is alive and of permanent value. **Moreover, conserving and giving continuity to elements of the past always involves renewing them, recreating them, integrating them into the new reality under construction, and in this sense improving them and bringing them to their full development**. The innovative force, if it is real, would not exist if it did not come

117

from the past, if it were not in some sense a thing of the past, that of the past which is alive and developing. This itself is conservation and innovation, and contains everything of past civilizations that is worthy of preservation and development.

However, the new civilization will only be really new and superior if it goes beyond the past, if it takes individual and social human experience towards unknown horizons. The new civilization is a new social order, and creating it implies introducing substantial novelty in individual and social life, which means that the transformation process must be much deeper and more extended than the changes which could be anticipated from reformist and revolutionary political viewpoints.

Such a radical transformation can only be the result of creative activity, that is, of activities and processes involving the introduction of new and original forms and content –that previously did not exist- in personal and social reality. Indeed, the only thing that can profoundly change what exists is **to create and implement new realities within the current reality**, that question what exists and by questioning cause it to be restructured. The main and decisive transforming activity is creative activity, that which is capable of **introducing effective historical novelties.**

Reformist and revolutionary policies have been characterized by reorganizing, with greater or lesser intensity, what already exists. The new creative politics of a superior civilization is not limited to reorganize, reform and revolutionize what already exists, but spreads by creating and introducing historical novelty which, interacting with the realities of the past change them profoundly, creating novel historical rationalities.

The most radical and profound change is the creation of the new; in this case creating new ways of thinking and living, new ways of doing economics and politics, new expressions of art, knowledge and spirituality, new ways of living together and social interaction, at the family, local, national, international and global levels.

XXV.

On the political project: Is it utopian or realistic? Who prepares the project? How are the goals and means established?

The transformative dimension of the new policy is reflected in the project that guides and directs it. It seeks to transform the present social reality, to take it to a new historical situation; that is the political project. This project, in terms of the change towards a new civilization, is a project of profound transformation of economic structure, social organization, of political institutions, cultural life, etc.

The first stage in any political project is to formulate goals and objectives to be achieved over a long period of time. It must also include an indication of the objectives and goals to be achieved in the medium and short term, as stages of a path leading to the desired end result. The project also involves identifying the necessary means for its realization; any political project must establish a relationship between means and goals.

In the politics of the old modern civilization the project has been defined in a number of ways. One way is an initial and permanent assumption of a certain theoretical 'model' of society, which must be 'applied' and implemented by the subjects 'sensitized' to the project. This 'model' fixes what is considered the 'must be' of the society to be built, some of which is derived from an ethical conception or social doctrine that reconciles what is considered fair, humane, natural, necessary, rational, and so on. In other cases the 'model' is derived from an ideology which expresses the interests of a class or social, religious or other group, which is supposed to be the bearer of the general interest of society. In both cases, the project has little to do with the analysis of the current reality and the specific characteristics of those apparently called to undertake the project. What the agents of change 'should' do is to be 'aware' of the 'model' and become the means and instruments for implementing it.

All social projects defined in this way have been utopian and unrealistic. The reason is clear: when you try to 'apply' a theoretical model in practice, that is to shape the whole social reality into an ideal 'model' developed by a few people, you inevitably generate antagonistic forces, since there other ways of thinking, other organizations and different interests, which deploy forces and opposition to the project that seek different results than those which the group carrying the 'model' wishes to implement. And the result is always something that creates a conflict that tends to be permanent.

The best that can be hoped for in this path is to materialize, for a historically short period of time, something like a distorted caricature of the ideal sought, and this based on a brutal dominating force -ideological, political and /or military- controlled by one group, that is imposed on others. This is because to change and reorganize a whole society according to a previously defined 'model', you need to have and use a lot of power, an immense power wielded and used by those who are the bearers and implementers of this 'model'. But having too much power supposes concentrating and accumulating, which can be achieved only to the extent that many others are stripped of their own ability to make decisions.

Therefore, the social transformation conceived as the application of a theoretical 'model' of society is not only infeasible, but also questionable from an ethical standpoint. That one or more social subjects, who can only be a part of society, consider themselves as carriers of a global project under which all society must be remodeled, supposes from the beginning that they are the exclusive possessors of the truth and appropriate values.

If by contrast we assume that truth and values are socially distributed and that no one has all the answers, that all persons and groups have ideas, values, interests and aspirations which may be legitimate and are entitled to exist; that social homogeneity is an impoverishment of human experience, and instead that diversity and pluralism are assets and are the product of the creative freedom of people, then we discover that it is not possible or appropriate to consider a transformation project understood as the application in practice of a 'model' of society developed by a few.

The need to think differently about social transformation becomes evident.

The criticism of those ways of understanding the transformation project cannot, however, lead us to adopt the other way of doing politics, also very typical of the modern civilization in crisis, which can be called pragmatic. Pragmatic politics always begins with an analysis of the present situation, but the purpose of political action vanishes, and politics is reduced to managing the existing reality. This type of politics is often called 'realistic', as opposed to the 'idealist' character of the previous mode. But the truth is that under such 'realism' hides the fact that pragmatic politics abandons transforming action, because it abandons the definition of goals and objectives, and activities are centered at the level of the media with regard to goals or objectives which are passively assumed, that are not consciously developed, because it is assumed that they are given, predetermined by the prevailing system.

Only the definition of goals through autonomous thinking activity may produce truly transformative activity. However, when the goals are already determined no real transformation is possible. The identification of new goals or objectives that transcend the rationality inherent in the expiring civilization is the beginning of a truly transformative action. But the definition of goals is not the formulation of an ideal 'model', of a 'must be' of society deductively derived from abstract principles.

Then what are the objectives of the new transformative politics, and how are they formulated?

The first thing that must be said is that those who assume the creation of a new and superior civilization must propose the goals and objectives to be achieved by them. In this sense they are maximally realistic and practical; they are obliged to make these goals considering the existing conditions, their own real capacity for action, their own energy and desire to achieve them. The overall objectives are not formulated for 'someone' - or 'others' - to put into practice.

However, to propose achievable, long, medium and short-term goals, the carriers of the transformative project do not have only their current capabilities and forces, since included in their own project is the goal of expanding their own capabilities, and also to invite, convoke and motivate the skills and energies of all the other people and existing organizations that can join the transforming project. Thus the project, along with the continuous integration of new strengths, also integrates new objectives and goals which become shared by all who may potentially be involved in its realization. The project is thus expansive, a multiplier of the energy required for its realization.

Thus goals will be designed in relation to the forces that are **potentially** available, and with the existing premises and situations, but understood **dynamically**. The new politics oriented to create a new civilization is based on effective reality, because reality can only be changed with reality; however, reality is not understood as something static or in a stable equilibrium, but as a set of individual and social subjects and human forces who can establish goals and projects to be achieved by their own will and conscious activity. Starting from this existing reality, in which there are subjects and progressive forces able to share the objectives which they are invited to achieve, a transformative project will be configured that will continue to expand, and reality will be transformed to the extent to which they achieve the goals which compose the project.

One wonders even more specifically, what is the reality which is pertinent to consider to establish the goals of transformation? How we do to understand it? And based on which aspects or elements of that reality we can formulate the objectives of its transformation?

These questions are crucial to differentiate the new politics from pragmatic politics, which also claims to be based on reality and on political realism. Indeed, **the analysis of the reality on which the formulation of the project in the new politics is based is developed through this new structure of knowledge mentioned above, or in those sciences which we define as 'critical' and 'comprehensive', which see historical reality as shaped by all the individuals who build it and who put into it all their subjectivity and their interactions, including the ethics and values that guide their actions, the interests and passions that motivate them and which configure the relations of the social forces that will determine the course of history.**

From this point of view, what is most interesting for the purpose of developing the project, identifying the goals and means of transformation, is the understanding of the new emerging economic, political and cultural **rationalities**, which may be **enhanced** through the political action of those who propose the project of the new civilization.

The starting point will be the recognition of the existing active subjects, and in particular those who act oriented in certain directions that potentially converge with the project of a new civilization, and who can be motivated and empowered to propose wider aims and objectives which are coherent and may be integrated into the great project. As these subjects (people, organizations, communities, networks, etc.) develop based on their particular objectives interact with those who propose the broader project of the new civilization, they will expand the field of their possible consciousness and will be progressively oriented toward the prospect of the new civilization, thus they will come to think, to propose and carry out broader and deeper objectives.

XXVI.

In which is analyzed the question of the State in the new civilization: the role it may occupy and the transformations that it will have to undergo.

Another key issue we need to think about with respect to the 'new politics' is that of the State. We have seen that the State is the 'unifying form' of modern civilization, being the central axis of its political pillar. If we propose to move to a new and higher civilization, it is worth asking whether the State will continue to be valid in it, and if the answer is yes, under what conditions its presence and activity will not imply maintaining politics trapped in the logic of modern decaying and perishing civilization.

I have said that the history of civilization shows that between one civilization and the next there is not a rupture or complete separation, but rather many elements of the previous civilization remain current and active in the new civilization. But the question I raised is not about just any element, but about the 'unifying form', which by definition is what centrally defines a civilization. It would be expected, then, that since State is the central 'unifying form' of modern civilization, it would cease to be so in the emerging new civilization.

It should be noted that this would not be the first time the 'unifying form' of a civilization remains in effect and active in the new civilization, although no longer operating as a central 'unifying form', but reduced to an element or particular component, and as such, subordinate and to a certain degree degraded, when it is integrated into the new civilization that replaces it. This was, for example, the case of the Catholic Church, which from having been the 'unifying form' of medieval European civilization, continues to function in modern civilization in which it is the State that has assumed the central quality of the 'unifying form'.

Based on this historical precedent, and thinking that the State fulfills some important functions that should continue in the new civilization, we can hypothesize that **the State will continue to be present in the new civilization, but no longer fulfilling the role of the 'unifying form'; stripped of its attributes of centrality, small in its functions, subordinate to a new central organizing component of social and political life, and also thoroughly reformed, transformed internally.**

Consider what this might mean and how it can be made to happen.

Based on everything I have discussed so far, especially that referring to the subjects who will be the creators of the new civilization, the dimensions and shape of its expansion, the mode of development of its own 'unifying form' and the characteristics of the new policy, I can advance some important conclusions about the changes that the State should experience in the transition to the new civilization.

First, the creation of the new civilization should imply a **substantial reduction of State power and functions.** On one hand, the recovery of control over their own living conditions by the people, organizations, networks and local communities means that many of the functions and activities that in current modern civilization have been concentrated in the State will be decentralized and disseminated socially. We may say that the State will experience, in this sense, a certain 'emptying from below'. Education, health, provision of local services, entertainment, retirement, mutual aid, and many other aspects necessary for the development of human life and social life will experience a significant decentralization process; **individuals, families and local communities will recover a set of functions and activities that have been concentrated in the State** and have made society unfairly centralized, bureaucratic and homogeneous.

This is coherent with the criterion of development and establishment of the new 'unifying form' which comes from the bottom up; that is, it conforms to the principle that people can do everything; thus smaller communities and local groups must do things themselves using their own abilities, while that which requires the assistance of a higher level instance will be assumed by the higher level social entities that are created for that purpose. Thus the process of social organization will gradually ascend to higher societal levels and finally to the universal level, which will take care of what can only be properly resolved at these higher levels.

In this way power, instead of being concentrated in the State will be socially diffused, allowing each creative, independent and solidary person, group and community, at their respective levels, to take charge of what they can satisfactorily perform, which will effectively give them power. As a result, human society will be articulated as a community of communities, an organization of organizations, a network of networks.

Additionally, considering that the new civilization is projected to planetary or universal dimensions, there will be aspects and functions which currently are fulfilled by the State - apparently but not really on behalf of the whole society, given its specific territorial characteristics - that will move to universal instances; that will be really an expression of humanity. This process may be viewed as an 'emptying' of the State 'from above'.

In this second sense we can think, for example, that nation States should be stripped of the ability to make war or their existing national armies be disbanded, for the common good of humanity and civilization requires peace between nations, and it has obviously been the availability of armies under the control of States which has made possible so many disastrous fratricidal wars between nations in the current civilization.

There should be a single instance which groups all nations, in which all have adequate representation and participation, which will have the military capacity to prevent one nation from rising up against another and to assure world peace preventing the establishment of relationships of dominance of the stronger and oppression of the weaker.

Another item that has been proven harmful to the existence of a just social order among nations has been the monopoly the modern national States have had over the issuance and control of money. A just economic order would require international business transactions not to be carried out using one or a few 'banknotes' issued and controlled by one or a few powerful States, with which unequal terms of trade are imposed on other countries. It is essential to have a single currency, one currency worldwide for trade and international finance, which must be issued and controlled by a single entity in which all nations have adequate representation and participation. At the same time, 'from below' it will be possible and desirable to for local currencies to appear, community and complementary currencies of the common people, to facilitate trade and promote local, community and communal development.

In addition to the reduction and relative 'emptying' of its now over-concentrated powers, the State will require profound transformation processes towards its real and effective **democratization**, in order **to expand citizen participation in decision-making processes.**

For one thing, for the reasons discussed above political parties would no longer be part of the structure of the State; they would not select the managers of the State or be the representation of groups, classes or particular categories. As a consequence, politics and the State would not function in a condition of permanent conflicts of interest and contrasting ideologies.

The necessary mediation between citizens and the central government would not be done by political parties; organizations, communities, networks and other groups that people form in civil society would have direct participation in a State set up as an organization of organizations, as a community of communities, as a network of networks.

The indirect representation of individuals characteristic of democracies in current modern civilization, which inevitably involves the division between rulers and ruled, would be replaced in the new civilization by the direct involvement of communities and other organizations that have been generated in civil society which would occur in decision-making and consultative bodies, which would dispense with permanent bureaucracies that are typical of current States in crisis. In the new forms of States, specialized technical functions and specialists which these functions might require would be under the control of citizens and their communities.

I leave here these reflections and ideas about the State in the new civilization; it should be clear that what has been stated so synthetically represents only provisional hypotheses, coherent and consistent with what has been said so far about the new politics. Because, as with the other dimensions of the new civilization, the forms and contents that States will assume will be conceived, designed, created and perfected by the same creative, autonomous and solidary subjects who build it.

What is clear is that the State will undergo profound changes in the process of creating the new civilization. These changes will be the result of the process of creating the new politics within civil society, which - as we saw earlier - will also be a political society, but without creating political power which rises above society and imposes on it.

XXVII.

Nations, peoples, ethnic and national communities in the creation of the new civilization.

Now reaching the end of these reflections on the new politics, I will address the question of nations and nationalities. This question is related to the issue of State examined in the previous presentation but is clearly different, so it is necessary to examine it to reveal its importance in the transition to a new civilization. Although many modern States have a national basis and are often characterized as national states, nations and States are not identical concepts.

When we speak of nations we refer to large historical-social units, to human communities which in successive generations over time have formed a cultural identity. In this sense the term 'nation' may be restrictive; it must be understood that by 'nations' I refer to different historical realities that are known by different names; thus a 'nation' includes, for example, original peoples of Latin America who have retained their cultural identity for centuries and also to the 'nationalities' which have their own languages and persist within several

European countries, along with various 'ethnicities' that characterize the complex African social groups, and other names with which people often identify with their culture and their own historical continuity.

The determinant of what is here understood as a 'nation' is the cultural identity and sense of historical continuity that generates among its members a strong sense of belonging, a sense of shared identity which is transmitted from generation to generation. These are collective units that have been generated through processes of long duration and extended range, in which certain numerous human populations have formed a culture, language, traditions, lifestyles and a collective memory that gives them a sense of historical continuity. Often nations are based on similar ethnic roots, similar world views or widely distributed religious beliefs in geographically defined territorial areas, but these elements are not necessarily present in all nations.

States, however, are usually formed by constituent acts of power exercised from situations of power, and integrate existing human settlements within a clearly demarcated territory with limits considered 'sovereign' which they defend with arms. States submit these settlements to a certain centralized political and military power, and a set of institutions and laws whose compliance is imposed on all inhabitants of the territory.

In synthesis, nations refer to civil societies while States refer to political societies. Nations came before States. And it has happened too often in modern civilization that States are not established on a national basis but are imposed on more than one nation, integrating several in an authoritarian manner. It has also happened that States have been defined territorially, dividing previously established nations.

In virtually all cases where a State was not established on a national basis, with borders which did not correspond to the extension of its institutional government and power, the emergence of conflicts and wars has been inevitable, both civil wars that manifest themselves within a State and wars between States seeking to extend their limits. Most of the wars and conflicts that have occurred and continue to occur in modern civilization have their origin in the lack of correspondence between the two instances mentioned, the civil nations and the political States.

The problem is particularly acute in cases where the formation of the State unit has been imposed authoritatively upon various nations, trying to submit them and to generate a new supranational collective identity. These States have often tried to create a so-called 'patriotic' identity, using the idea of a fatherland to generate a cultural identity over bases that are not national and do not have deep historical roots. In other words, with the idea of 'fatherland' States have sought to supplant previous national identities and to create a patriotic feeling to disrupt or undermine national collective pasts whose geographical areas do not match the state's territorial boundaries.

It must be noted that in the transition to the new civilization, this source and foundation of so many conflicts and wars should disappear, since in the new civilization States would lose their power over the nations, since the latter will recover their autonomy, and there will be recognition of the presence and participation of nations in international and world bodies. In both ways, nations -- peoples, ethnic, national communities, nationalities, etc. -- will also be protagonists in the creation of the new civilization.

However, in modern civilization it has often happened that nations subjected to state entities that control them have adopted forms of political action that are not part of their cultural traditions but are really from the civilization of States, leading to nationalist and independence political movements that exert their action even by violent means. Beyond the debate over the legitimacy or illegitimacy of such forms of political action (which could be discerned by considering the degree of oppression and destruction that the States that dominate them have forced and continue to force on them), it is important to understand that a real and definite end to the conflicts and their causes can be achieved only in the process of creating a new, post-State civilization which recognizes and values local and national communities and that integrates them harmoniously into a new universal identity .

As part of this process, what nations do to regain their identities, their languages, their cultures, their music, their art, customs and traditions is important, getting rid of the incrustation of the foreign forms of politics they have acquired as a an effect of their subordinated integration into a modern State civilization.

It must also be understood that the new civilization looks to the future and opens up new forms of knowledge, culture, thought and art, and new ways of doing economics and politics, superior to those which humanity has experienced and known so far, and therefore also superior to those that nations have had in the past. In this regard, national realities will grow in creativity, autonomy and solidarity when they integrate into the creative processes of the new civilization, as will all individual and collective subjects who will shape the new civilization.

The 'unifying form' of a new and higher civilization is not the State, but it is not the nation, either. What is important is to recognize that nations, communities and ethnic groups, by themselves and independently of the States, will have their recognized place and their special contribution to make in the creation of a new social order and new dynamics of transformation, development and improvement of human experience. Thus it is crucial and essential to understand that the new 'unifying form' will not destroy minor social formations or be built by denying the diversity and plurality of national and ethnic cultures, but will enhance them and even enrich them by incorporating the dynamics of the fundamental values of creativity, autonomy and solidarity, in the terms and the meanings that we have understood.

Employing their own creativity, autonomy and solidarity, nations or indigenous peoples, nationalities, historical communities and ethnic groups will be important creators of the new civilization. Recovering their values, their cultures, their technologies, their knowledge and their own identities, they will help to enrich the new civilization with concepts that they have preserved or rescued, many of them coming from civilizations prior to modern times, which can contribute wisdom, experience and community and human richness that in the future will be shared with all humanity.

This concludes the reflections on the new politics, and we are prepared to begin the analysis of the new economy.

.

XXVIII.

Here we begin to discuss the new economy, addressing the issue of funding and resources for initiatives and projects.

As a way to move from reflection on the new politics to the equally important issue of the new economy that is to characterize the civilization we want to build, I will start with a very specific and concrete subject, the resources and financing that are needed for the implementation of initiatives, activities and projects of the creation of the new civilization. Initiatives must be financed; funding is necessary to carry out the work that the participants in the project intend to do. All initiatives and organizations must spend money, perform jobs, use materials, devote time to management, maintain systems, etc. Although this a very specific item, by examining it we will see ideas and elements appear which may illuminate important aspects of the new economy and the new civilization, considered in its broadest sense.

In the civilization of the State and organizations that concentrate power and maintain bureaucratic structures, its

137

members are required to pay regular amounts of money (taxes, duties, contributions, fees) that are collected by the governing center, with which it finances the activities of the organization or State. This will not be the way the creators and participants of the new civilization contribute resources to the development of the project. Indeed, this way of financing projects has two undesirable effects for the new civilization: 1. It reinforces the power of the central body (the leaders); and 2. It weakens and subordinates the contributors (the led). This is part of a mode of relationship between leaders and led which corresponds to the civilization in crisis, and must also be overcome.

The mode of financing based on obligatory taxes and tariffs is necessary where the State is separated from society and has established itself as an exterior power which governs. Under these conditions individuals and intermediate groups are not able to obtain resources freely; they do not participate in determining the activities which are carried out by those who control power.

The new civilization is based on the creativity, autonomy and solidarity of its participants. Therefore, instead of being obliged to deliver the resources to the central collection center that will decide hierarchically to which activities it will allocate the proceeds, the citizens of the new civilization will freely provide resources in proportion to their own commitment, to fund the initiatives, activities and works that they decide to undertake, and also those of others that they want to support and encourage.

This applies to all levels which will be produced in the new civilization, from the personal to the local, national and global levels. Each level has its own functions and projects to finance and participants at each level will provide the resources they consider necessary and appropriate for its realization.

This begins with the individual level, on which I will now focus the reflection. If we are citizens of the new civilization, everything we do with our money and resources which contributes to our own development and autonomy, our own growth and improvement, and complies with the guidelines of the new civilization, is a contribution to its creation and expansion. This applies to individuals and groups, organizations, communities and networks, and to an organization of organizations, community of communities, network of networks, etc. To grow, expand self-realization, satisfy needs, aspirations and complete the projects that we carry out as participants in this new civilization at any level is a contribution to it, and will also have the effect of attracting, motivating and incorporating those who value positive growth and accomplishments.

From the personal viewpoint, acting economically in the context of the new and superior civilization will probably mean that we stop spending according to the logic of the old civilization, and establish spending and consumption priorities very different from those we currently have as inhabitants the old modern civilization.

In the new civilization no one tells us on what we should spend our money, what to consume, how to use our resources. Each autonomous participant also becomes autonomous in this, to the degree to which she/he becomes aware of how many and which options are adopted in dependence and subordination to the criteria of the old civilization (usually induced by the leaders, publicity and the State), and how many and which consumer habits he/she decides to change to strengthen their own autonomy, creativity and solidarity, in order to participate in the great project.

Participation in the new civilization leads to great changes in habits and consumption patterns, and to formulate a new structure of needs, aspirations and projects. This will probably involve allocating fewer resources to those types of consumption that are characteristic of the old civilization and reproduce it, which will free up resources to be used to strengthen the new civilization.

We will probably have to abandon the over-consumption, consumerism, imitative consumption, compulsive consumption, status and ostentatious consumption which are characteristic of modern civilization in crisis. We must also reverse the trend to borrow to have quicker access to certain consumer goods that we can do without. We will probably also eliminate or reduce our cost structure in certain types of donations that generate dependency in the beneficiaries. Critical analysis of the customs and habits of consumption and expenditure acquired according to the logic of the civilization in crisis will surely indicate to us many items to delete in our budgets.

This will allow us to have the means to carry out initiatives that will make us more independent, creative and supportive. Beginning with one self, we must devote more resources, time and means, for example to study, learning and the expansion of knowledge; to personal development and the extension of our relations, extension of conviviality; to creative activities, etc. We will learn to entertain ourselves in new ways, to organize our time in other ways, to spend on the acquisition of resources and goods and services that will provide access to increasing levels of autonomy, creativity, knowledge, relationship, community and organization.

But we have proposed a large task -- to start creating a new civilization. This will require self-organization, networking, and deployment of a multitude of initiatives and projects in the most varied fields of economics, politics, culture and science. And all these organizations, networks, initiatives and projects require resources to develop. Since these are our own initiatives, our projects, our networks and organizations, we are the ones really interested in financing them. If the project is our project, if the network is our network, if its development is our need, aspiration and desire, we will not have problems in dedicating the money, time, labor and resources required to perform them and allow them to achieve their objectives. No one decides for us, thus we should not expect others to fund what we propose to do freely and autonomously.

In this respect we are spoiled, because in the decaying civilization we finance the central power, the State, and then ask the State to provide us the funding we require for our purposes. This approach is not consistent with the new civilization, since it reproduces the dependence and subordination of the ruled by the rulers, of the subjects by the powerful, and concentrates power and wealth.

However, in the task of initiating the creation of a new civilization we are not alone, as we can count on the reinforcements, contributions, funds and aid provided to us by other people participating in the same large project who have resources available and contribute because they value what we are doing. Similarly, we are available to assist the initiatives of other people, networks, communities and organizations whose projects and achievements we appreciate. As was said before, the new civilization requires autonomous people who are also solidary. Organizations, communities and autonomous networks must also be solidary.

The ways of identifying projects to be undertaken and their modes of financing will be different at each level of the organization process of the new arising civilization, but at each level decisions will be made by the responsible participants, with creativity, autonomy and solidarity. Later I will return to the issue of financing and marketing initiatives in the economy of the new civilization, because there is much more to say on this subject.

XXIX.

Which explains the limited success of many 'non-capitalist' and 'alternative' economic experiences, and why the creation of a new economy must start with consumption.

A new civilization includes creating a new economy. We broached the subject recognizing the existence of multiple and varied initiatives, experiences and processes oriented in ways that may converge in the project of a new civilization, and then can be enhanced when wider aims and objectives are proposed and consciously integrated into the great project. Those who develop those experiments - people, organizations, movements, communities, networks, etc. - create and operate them according to their own objectives, but may expand their consciousness and objectives in the perspective of the new civilization.

The fact is that the search for a new economy, an alternative to the capitalist and statist economy has been pursued for a long time. Attempts to create a new economy based on autonomy, creativity and solidarity of its participants have been many and varied. Among them we can mention cooperatives, self-management, communitarian economy, the economy of communion, fair trade, ethical finance, responsible consumption, popular economic organizations, and several others.

These movements have reached a certain level of interesting development; they are valuable as evidence of the possibility of an economy ethically superior to capitalism. But we must recognize that they have not been sufficient to overcome capitalism and statism, and largely remain subordinate to the logic of modern civilization. A question that must then be asked is, what has prevented their further development, or what inherent limits do they have that have not allowed them to establish a truly new and superior economy?

The question is important, because if it were external constraints or hitherto insurmountable obstacles that the dominant powers in modern civilization have imposed, we might conclude that we already have the new economic forms and that it is only necessary to expand them and develop them, framing them in broader transformation processes that would eliminate the obstacles that these attempts have had. But if there are internal limits, problems that are unique to these movements that have prevented their deployment and expansion, we would still need to find better answers to the question about new and improved ways of organizing economics.

We are aware that in many circumstances the non-capitalist, cooperative and self-managed economic organizations have faced obstacles placed by laws and especially by the strong capitalist concentration in which the market operates. However, in many countries and conditions these attempts have enjoyed broad moral consensus with respect to the validity of their objectives, and sufficient support by state and government bodies, who have helped with legal support, tax privileges, technical and financial assistance. This leads me to think that we must look at issues inherent in their way of organization, relations and actions to find the major constraints to their development.

Perhaps the most serious problem with these alternative experiments is the fact that so far, apart from being ethically superior, they have not proved to be also more efficient from the economic standpoint, i.e. that they make more productive use of resources which provide better returns for people involved in them and achieve more convenient conditions of price and quality of goods and services for consumers.

To explain or justify this, the argument is often used that economic efficiency must be sacrificed in order to achieve a socially just economy and more human and superior ethical values. The problem is that an inefficient economy cannot expand and grow beyond certain limits, because most people (entrepreneurs, workers, consumers, savers, etc.) are not willing to sacrifice their own utilities based on purely ideological or ethical requirements The usual discourse of the promoters of these "alternative" economies almost always includes a call to sacrifice; you have to sacrifice for the common good, to sustain the "social" project, you must be willing to pay more for "ethical" products, etc.   But the economy, by definition, is aimed at producing net benefits, in the sense that the benefits must always be greater than the sacrifices, and the economy will be more attractive and efficient as the benefits are greater and the sacrifices smaller. Thus a new socially superior economy cannot expand to the point where it can prevail unless it is simultaneously more ethical (fair, supportive, free) and more efficient.

Years ago I wrote a book *("Workers' Enterprises and Market Economy")* to examine the historical reasons for the limited success of "alternative economic projects ". I will summarize here the most important causes of these limits:

First: **They have been based on unrealistic notions about "human nature".** In some cases they have assumed that people are naturally generous and caring, putting little emphasis on the need for personal development in terms of creativity, autonomy and solidarity. In other cases they have ignored legitimate personal and family interests, based on a collectivist view of society.

Second: **Lack of a theoretical and scientific development to understand, enhance and guide the organization and economic development of those experiments**. It is true that cooperatives, self-management, community economy, fair trade, ethical finance, responsible consumption, etc. have principles and thoughts that guide them, but they are essentially of a doctrinal or ideological, regulatory and ethical type, not based on economic science, and do not correspond to the new structure of knowledge that I have argued to be necessary to start creation of a new and higher civilization.

Third: **They have remained at the "primitive" levels of rupture (staying out) and antagonism (working against)** the economic theories and practices of modern economy, without rising to the necessary level of autonomy. The consequence is that these experiments are usually self-defined in negative rather than affirmative terms, as shown in the expressions "non-profit", "non-capitalist" and the fact that they do not recognize the market as the socially necessary place to confront the other forms of economic organization.

Fourth: A particular issue that so far has limited and made difficult the creation of supportive economic initiatives has been **giving privilege to and emphasizing the organization and activities of production and distribution over those of consumption**. In fact, the main processes aimed at creating a new economy have usually started by creating productive, commercial and financial initiatives. This is probably an ideological legacy of Marxism, which emphasizes this and makes it prevail over consumption and satisfaction of human needs in its economic concept of production and distribution.

With these critical considerations we are not disqualifying cooperatives, self-management, community economy, ethical finance, fair trade and many other experiments and related movements. They are real components, even essential for the creation of the new civilization. What I claim is that they must overcome the limitations that they have demonstrated so far, undergo an in-depth renovation and achieve increasing degrees of autonomy, creativity and solidarity, so that by assuming fully the objectives and the project of a new civilization they fulfill their potential and reach the level of consciousness - theoretical and practical - required to be effective in the realization of this great project.

More specifically, a conceptual reformulation process is required to guide in overcoming these limitations. This formulation should include, first of all, a more thorough and accurate conception of 'human nature' and the needs of man and society.

The development of a comprehensive economic theory is also required, based on the new structure of knowledge that I have indicated as appropriate for the creation of the new civilization, and that will allow a better understanding of the economic rationalities of the new economy in the areas of consumption, distribution and production.

There must also be a new conception of development, i.e. processes of expansion and improvement of the new economy that are ecologically sustainable in relation to the requirements of the environment; that are socially and politically consistent and realistic and provide clear and convincing guidelines for individuals and organizations focused on the perspective of the new civilization.

I will examine these ideas in the following chapters.

XXX.

It begin to analyze consumption and why the vast majority of consumers are currently passive, dependent and competitive.

In creating a new economy the starting point is the transformation of consumption. The reason is clear: if we assume that the objective of the new economy is human beings, their fulfillment and happiness, we must begin by examining whether the consumption of goods and services produced in the economy is serving that purpose, which basically involves meeting the actual needs of human beings. This is because consumption consists of satisfying the needs of individuals and society through the goods and services produced in the economy.

The consumption of a food occurs in the act of eating it, satisfying the need for nourishment and the enjoyment of its taste. A book is consumed when it is read, to satisfy the desire to learn and to enjoy reading. The consumption of a medical therapy occurs in the process of healing the disease and becoming healthy.

This has not been understood in the current modern economy; in the so-called 'consumer theory' consumption is reduced to the behavior of people in the market in buying goods and services. From this perspective the consumption of food occurs at the supermarket, the consumption of a book is the purchase of the book, the therapy would be consumed when you pay for it. So it doesn't matter if the food nourishes the person well, or the book makes her/him more cultured, or if the therapy heals and makes the person happy. What matters is how much money consumers spend on the purchase.

Economic theories have not addressed the essence of the economy, which is meeting the needs and development of people; what interests them is that individuals are in the market and buy as much as possible; it may even be better if people remain unsatisfied, if it compels them to buy more things and services.

It requires a new conception of consumption to design and build a new and superior economy. But then it is necessary to rethink completely the question of need, based on criticism of the way we conceive it in modern society. This criticism is necessary to understand the radical change we need to make at the level of consumption. Because – we may anticipate – it is the current pattern of consumption which leads people to feel their needs in a way that makes them passive, dependent and competitive. This will be radically different from the consumption that makes us creative, autonomous and supportive; but this new mode of consumption involves understanding human needs in a different way.

In modern civilization there have been two ways of understanding needs: the liberal-capitalist and social-statist; although these are in opposition at the political level, both are based on a similar positivist and naturalist idea of man and society.

According to the liberal-capitalist conception human nature is not common to all men; there are only individuals who behave empirically in certain ways, each with his/her own particular interests, needs and desires; each vying with the others. Human needs are those that individuals express in their demands for goods and services on the market.

Needs are conceived as lacks or desires, as gaps to be filled with goods and services, so there would kind of bi-univocal correspondence between needs and products and services. Each need corresponds to a product, and each product corresponds to a need. Thus needs are not felt as personal needs, but as the needs of buying and owning things and services. It is further assumed that needs are recurrent, i.e. that they are satisfied every time the gaps are filled with products; but these soon reappear unsatisfied, and therefore goods and services are always in demand to satisfy them for a while, until the empty gaps or needs appear again.

Along with these recurrent needs, it is supposed that needs are growing. Once human beings meet certain needs, we always desire to satisfy other, new, broader and more sophisticated needs, thus we are always dissatisfied. It says that we are insatiable. And since needs are expanding, multiplying and diversifying, the economy is also multiplying and diversifying the products, i.e. the goods and services it offers.

But are human beings really like this? Are we a species with many needs, with so many empty compartments which are filled and emptied, which are multiplying and growing, and always demanding more goods and services to be fulfilled? Or is that just how the capitalist market wants us to be?

Another view of needs that has been present in current modern civilization is the social-statist, which gave rise to the centrally planned economy. The conception of man underlying this concept is that initially postulated by Ludwig Feuerbach and later developed by Marx and Engels, in which all that could be associated with the idea of human nature would be the collective group, understood as the natural human 'species'.

This concept continues to conceive of needs as recurring gaps that are filled with increased products and services; but differs from the liberal conception that makes a clear distinction between those which would be 'real' human needs -those characteristic of the species - and those which would only individual desires and whims. The 'true needs' would be common and equal for everyone: food, clothing and shelter, housing, protection, information and knowledge, health services and few more.

Since there are few easily identifiable needs which may be put in a hierarchy in their social importance, it is claimed that you can plan for increasing satisfaction through State action. Each society could define its needs, but as a group; it is society that could determine the needs at all times which can and should be fulfilled. Therefore, according to this conception, the economy must be planed and regulated strictly, reducing the free spaces in which individuals express their desires and whims, because if individuals persist in expressing their demands freely, planning would not be possible.

The difference between the liberal-capitalist and social-statist conception is that while in the former products to meet needs are demanded by individuals and provided by the market, in the latter the products are determined and provided by the State.

These two conceptions of needs even though politically opposite, in practice have been amalgamated in modern society. On one hand it recognizes that individuals may freely express their demands for goods and services in the market. And on the other hand it is accepted that there is a level of access to certain goods and services which should be equal for all people that is understood as a 'right' who citizens may require of the State.

However, this recognition of both conceptions as legitimate results in a structure of demands, and a type of consumer, - that will be called the modern consumer - who is very demanding and complicated, which creates an economic problem that tends to be insoluble, and causes the great crisis that affects the current but old modern civilization.

Indeed, from both viewpoints (the capitalist market and the State provider) the needs are growing, multiplying and diversifying, and thus the economy is hard pressed to grow, to multiply the supply of goods and services to meet both the collective demands required from the State and the individual demands expressed in the market. From both perspectives, from both logics, we are experiencing an increase in the threshold of the quantity of products that are demanded and the expected level of access.

On one side is the logic of the market, which is primarily logic of individuation, a logic of differentiation by the possession of things, where everyone tries to differentiate themselves, to win prestige and to have access to more goods and services. Thus there is a kind of pursuit, because nobody wants to be left behind; those who have greater purchasing power require increasingly sophisticated and complex goods and services, and more of them. Those who follow them are accessing these levels with some delay; but the most advanced try to distinguish themselves, by acquiring more sophisticated, more refined products. And thus the market continues in a relentless pursuit.

At the same time, there is a persistent increase in the minimum level considered socially acceptable. Increases at the level of individuals generate an increase at the collective level, because others show off their increases, by the effect of imitation, by the effect of "well, why can't we have what others have?" Thus the State is required to provide its citizens with better living conditions, more and better modes of transport, better education systems, better health and protection services, access to education at ever higher levels, etc.

In turn, raising the level of what everyone has generates a market pressure to differentiate from above. For example: if everyone has a college education the market will generate instances for those who want to be more than the common and press for higher levels of education for their children. This happens in all areas of needs.

Thus the modern consumer, as well as being insatiable, is extremely exigent and demanding from the State, believing that she/he is entitled to have the State provide all that is needed to achieve the social average environment, and also entitled to have the market provide everything he wants and can afford. And if he cannot pay cash, he believes that he is entitled to be given the credit to buy it.

All this leads to an impressive acceleration process of demands, both individual and social. It is what we are experiencing today. And this expansion and explosion of the needs and demands on the market and on the State creates a huge strain on the production system. It generates a pressure to grow, i.e., to increase rapidly the production process of goods and services together with the rapid expansion of needs.

But it must be asked, is it possible to grow indefinitely? Will there be sufficient resources and capabilities to support this continued growth? If we continue along this path will the consequences it is having on the environment be reversible? And will it be possible to overcome the serious impacts that unrestrained consumerism is having on collective coexistence, governability, social ethics and cultural and spiritual values?

Moreover, is it not just because we are reaching the limits of the possible growth in consumption, which is now becoming evident in the organic crisis of modern civilization, that there is an urgent need to build a civilization with a different economy?

And the bottom line: Is it true that access to more products and services provides a better satisfaction of human needs, makes us become happier and perform better as individuals?

XXXI.

Showing that creative, antonomous and solidary consumption requires another way of thinking and living our needs.

Modern consumers are not a creative, autonomous and solidary consumer. On the contrary, their consumption is imitative, dependent and competitive. This is desired by the dominant political economy, the capitalist market and the welfare State. It is a consumption that diminishes people, and ultimately generates dissatisfaction and unhappiness, which seems to be the normal state of many people in the terminal phase of the crisis of modern civilization.

We must free ourselves from this imitative, dependent, compulsive and competitive consumption in order to have access to the autonomous, creative and supportive consumption corresponding to a new and higher civilization. Neither the market nor the State will make this change; it would be absurd to demand it from the market or the State, which are the drivers of dependent and passive consumption. The change in modes of consumption is only possible if we do it ourselves, everyone changing and creating a cultural change from our environment that will expand a new way of living our needs and consuming what is adequate for our personal and social development.

Autonomous consumption is that which is not guided by advertising or does not mimic the decisions made by others or compete to have more than the neighbors. Autonomous consumption also does not get carried away by personal desires and whims, which is rather a form of slavery which implies that we do not control our own existence freely and consciously.

Truly autonomous consumers are those who identify their goals looking for integral personal human fulfillment, satisfying real needs which are not indicated by the market and the State or by our immediate instincts, but those which we discover through consciousness of our human nature, of who we are and what we are oriented to be.

Thus we understand that all our needs fall into four broad dimensions of human experience that can be represented by two intersecting axes, or by four vectors that separate from a common point of origin.

The first (horizontal) axis is formed on one side by the vector of the needs we have as individuals: the need for safety and security, personal identity, achievement of our individual interests and projects. On the opposite side is the vector of needs as a community and society: the need for communication, interaction, participation, collective projects.

The second (vertical) axis is formed by the descending vector of physical and material needs: the need for food, health, housing, protection from the elements of nature, utensils and equipment, etc. The ascending vector represents cultural and spiritual needs; the need for knowledge, artistic expression, transcendence, beauty, goodness, truth, values and higher experiences.

Our fulfillment occurs in the progressive satisfaction of needs that present themselves in the processes of our expansion and development in these four dimensions of human experience. In these processes we use things and services that the economy provides, but the needs are fulfilled in ourselves due to our own actions, which take advantage of those things and services. This is the perspective that we must give to consumption, reversing the current situation that puts people at the service of things, muddling the rational relationship between means and ends.

In the perspective of this fulfilling consumption by people and communities, needs are not presented as gaps or voids to fill with objects, but as potentialities, as experiences that we can actively deploy. Needs are triggers for activities, initiatives and processes designed to make real that which exists potentially, virtually, in every individual and every group.

The possibility to create a new economic paradigm lies in the re-discovery of man as endowed with spirit, conscience and freedom, and consequently creative, independent and supportive, responsible for his/her actions. From this we can derive some details about specifically human needs.

The first is that we **experience needs at the level of consciousness**. Even bodily needs such as food and shelter are lived subjectively. In humans, everything happens and everything is lived consciously, i.e., simultaneously in the mind and the body, and in both planes we search to satisfy needs, which will always be some social or personal fulfillment.

Associated with this is the fact that our needs represent energy waiting to be deployed, **they are forces that seek to reveal themselves**. They are directional vectors in the sense that they actively seek some achievement, some result for the individual or the group. These are energies, but they are creative energies, capable of producing that which will satisfy them. This allows us to understand creativity in consumption.

I am talking about autonomous and creative consumption. Starting from the idea that a need is not satisfied solely by an external thing one possesses or the action that is accessed, but by the use the person gives to the thing or the external service, we discover **that the true satisfaction of the need is obtained through the deployment of the energy released by the need itself**. The need for food is not satisfied by the food, but by the activity of eating and obtaining nutrition. The need for knowledge is not satisfied by the information given to the person to memorize and learn passively, as though their ignorance were an empty space that requires filling, but through the active construction of knowledge, using as components input or knowledge and information that others have developed previously; an effect is only produced when this knowledge and information is rebuilt in their own learning process.

Moreover, needs have a process, which implies that more than simply recurring, as it is usually claimed, they are **progressively perfected**. For example, a person feels the need to read novels and poetry, listen to music, etc. These needs develop and perfect the extent that we read, listen to music and study. We develop our aesthetic needs as we observe (or better yet, create) paintings and sculptures, that is, as we become more educated.

Therefore, I conceive a consumption that leads us to satisfy our needs independently and creatively, improving our being. This is not only different from contemporary consumerism, but also from the idea that the only state of complete satisfaction that a person can obtain is by annulling her/his needs, which conceives of happiness as not feeling needs. If we think human needs as positive energy, we do not feel that is to reach that state of quenching of the needs, to desire nothing and thus be satisfied. Although humans can, with discipline and internal effort, turn off some of their needs, stop their action and somehow be "at peace" with themselves, that does not necessarily approximate the fulfillment of "human nature".

Needs are constructive forces in the sense that they are expressions of the potential of people, that we want to be more than we are. And this desire to be more than what we are sometimes produces dissatisfaction. But it is dissatisfaction with what we already are as a result of things previously achieved, and also allows us to be happy, to be satisfied with what we have accomplished. So this is not dissatisfaction with not having things or access to certain services, but the anxiety that results from feeling the call to be more, to expand our consciousness, to reach higher goals.

Dissatisfaction so understood leads us to conceive of need as a project. In fact, **human beings live needs as projects**. Even the need to eat includes the project of the lunch that we must prepare to meet that need. Needs motivate, impel and move us to be more, to perfect ourselves. Orienting our consumption with the object of fulfillment and personal and social development heads us towards a higher civilization, in which human experience can discover new horizons, perhaps even some hitherto unknown.

XXXII.

The qualities of good consumption, or how to make consumption a journey of personal fulfillment and development.

Once we have understood needs as specifically human, and defined the objectives of consumption in the four dimensions of our experience, we can still ask: How should we use goods and services so that their consumption will give us the greatest and best result for our personal and social fulfillment? We can identify a set of **'good qualities of consumption'**, which lead to a better quality of life using fewer goods and services, and somewhat different ones than those we buy now.

A first quality of good consumption is **'moderation'**, which does not mean austerity, deprivation or sacrifice. Moderation means that goods and services used in proportion to need. A surplus of goods and services or an immoderate use can generate an unmet need as strong as a shortage or lack of goods and services. Moderation means to adjust the amount of goods and services to the extent and intensity of needs.

A second quality of good consumption is the 'correspondence', that is, that for each need those goods and services that can satisfy it in the best way be chosen and used. For example, the need for entertainment can be satisfied in a number of ways; by a group game, a social gathering, by reading and listening to music, or by movie or watching television. There are many ways to satisfy every need. Good consumption tries to satisfy them with that item or service which best suits each need and that favors their human development. Finding this correspondence is something that each individual should do autonomously.

A third quality of good consumption is 'persistence', which means that the satisfaction of needs is so well accomplished that the effect is lasting and the need does not recur soon. Persistence depends very much on what goods and services we use, and how we consume them. If you nourish yourself adequately, if you read a good book, if you have fun in a healthy and pleasant way, satisfaction continues over time, thus freeing up time, resources and energies for other aspects of personal fulfillment.

A fourth quality of good consumption can be identified with the words 'integrity', 'balance' and 'harmony'. Taking into account that we are individuals who have multiple needs in each of the four dimensions of human development; by integrity, balance and harmony I mean that we should not use all our activities and energy in only one or a few dimensions of our experiences and needs, but address them all in harmony. The integrity, balance and harmony comes when we have the material things and have decided the time and actions we dedicate to different activities, without neglecting any of the four dimensions of human experience.

A fifth quality of good consumption may be called **'ranking'**, and refers to the choices we make in organizing the satisfaction of our needs in time, choosing to do some first and leaving others until the right time. Ranking means placing the process of meeting needs under control of the individual. Being manager of our own development, we make choices and plan the even the process of consumption. Obviously there are basic needs that we cannot neglect and require priority attention. And there are fundamental and superior needs due to the value they have in personal and group development which I also emphasize and give greater importance.

A sixth quality of good consumption which I will call **'empowerment'**, means that self-satisfaction of needs perfects, elevates and energizes them. If needs are energy, those needs which prompt us to do things, fulfill goals or undertake creative activities, we will seek to empower them in the process of satisfying them. If we always satisfy our cultural needs at a basic level we will stagnate; if we always read the same type of books and always listen to the same kind of music, we're not improving our ability to appreciate works of art and literature, so our need stagnates. Empowerment means trying to make the consumption process develop qualitatively those needs, making needs more and more properly human, more creative, more self-sufficient.

I will call a seventh quality of good consumption **'coordination and integration'**, which consists of combining the satisfaction of various needs through the simultaneous use of different goods and services. Contrary to the tendency to consume a product for every need, we can think that through a complex activity we can simultaneously satisfy different needs, especially if that complex activity is performed by a group. For example, in a community get-together we can satisfy simultaneously needs for relationship, interaction, information, communication, power, participation, protection and many others, generating great satisfaction and happiness.

The eighth quality of good consumption is identified with **'cooperation and reciprocity'**. If we aspire to integral human development, to a complex, rich and diversified experience, we will not likely do so individually. Individually we tend to concentrate on certain directions of experience, neglecting others. Integrated development requires participation in collectives, being part of families and communities living and sharing with other.

If one wants to develop spiritual needs or to improve their knowledge, it is useful to find other people who want the same thing; if you want to develop your musical or sports talent, you must connect with people who share these motivations. And if we participate in an organization, a human experience where there are people who excel in different qualities, all are enriched by being part of a group where we can learn much from each other.

It is especially rewarding to relate to autonomous, creative and solidary people that have reached a higher level of personal development. A musician or a scientist grows in the interaction with great musicians or scientists. Seeking autonomy, creativity and solidarity, we are attracted and driven by those who have come higher or further than us, and this happens in every area and moment of life. Those who have an overabundance of precious qualities often share them generously with those willing to receive them.

This relates to another aspect of the progressive autonomy of individuals and groups; when a need is less developed it is more dependent on external satisfaction. A child needs to be fed and to be taught; she/he does not develop spirituality alone. Put another way: the more a need is expressed as a lack, as empty (because it is still pure potentiality, because it still has not been updated), the more satisfaction depends on external things and the actions of others. As people increase their fulfillment, the satisfaction of needs becomes autonomous, requiring fewer external elements to satisfy them.

This puts us on the threshold of the subject of production, as an aspect also inherent in the new economy, which I will discuss in the next chapter.

XXXIII.

Good consumption makes profound changes in production indispensable, associated with making the productive process more subjective.

One conclusion from the previous analyses is that the best satisfaction of needs, access to a higher quality of life and personal and group fulfillment do not involve increasing purchases and consumption and do not necessarily require greater production. The obvious consequence of this is that good consumption, "enlightened" consumption, involves a radical transformation of production; it requires profound changes in two closely related aspects, in what is produced and how it is produced.

If we produce to satisfy human needs and development, much of current production and in particular many goods and services that satisfy consumerism and dependent, imitative and competitive consumption, will no longer be necessary or useful. A new structure of production will be created as more individuals and groups start adopting the principles of moderation, correspondence, persistence, integrity, balance, hierarchy, empowerment, integration and cooperation that are characteristic of good consumption.

In general terms I can predict that agriculture and the production of basic goods and services will expand, along with education and culture, communications and local services. By contrast, mining, heavy industry, transport, oil and its derivatives, chemicals, financial services, and the widespread production of trinkets may all be reduced. As a result both the environment and the quality of life will improve, generating a very different type of development than the current unsustainable economic growth. The economy and development in the new civilization will be socially and environmentally sustainable.

However, this will not be just a change in what is produced, but also in the ways and structures that productive activities will use. These transformations are a direct consequence of, on one hand, the expansion of creative, autonomous and supportive consumption that we have analyzed, and on the other hand of the implementation of the values and criteria of the social organization of the new civilization.

In correspondence with the new forms of consumption, there will be a process of empowerment of the production capabilities of people, families, communities and local groups. We saw that 'good consumption' leads people and communities from dependency to autonomy. This is a process, and indeed autonomy is possible after reaching a certain level of development. We can understand with an example. If someone has never read a book, the motivation to do this and to learn to read must come from the outside. But after you have become a reader, no one has to motivate you to read, by yourself you feel the need to read, seek books and may even write down your own stories and thoughts, offering them to others. The same goes for any activity or labor; **we can gradually move from dependency to autonomy and from autonomy to solidarity, to the extent that we develop the skills involved in the activity or work we do.**

It is poverty, insecurity, lack of skills, lack of relationships, the absence of convictions, which make the acquisition of things and the use of external services so esteemed. But when we reach a certain level of personal development we become more self-sufficient, less in need of goods and external services. Someone who has good personal development and a wealth of personality will most likely need to buy fewer goods and services, not because needs have been eliminated but because they are satisfied more autonomously, and because the person is more dedicated to those dimensions of experience in which he/she is capable of self-generating projects and satisfying need on her/his own.

Thus we can see that the new economy should include a great development of autonomous and associative labor, self-employment, self-production and local development processes. Along with this there will be a more direct relationship between consumption and production, including greater self-sufficiency in food and energy locally and nationally. This is all part of the growth in autonomy, creativity and solidarity of the individuals, families, organizations and communities.

While in modern economy there are few businessmen and many dependent workers, in the new economy we will all be oriented to be entrepreneurial, creative, autonomous and solidary. In these conditions, many companies will be created through the free association of people with different and complementary resources and capabilities who cooperate to achieve the economic goals they share. When companies are formed this way, it is not possible for exploitation and domination to occur, or the enrichment of a few at the expense the work and sacrifice of many. These new production units are formed, organized and operate on the principles of justice and fairness that characterize the solidary economy, which I will also call the **economy of solidarity, work and community**.

Looking deeper, we find that one of the fundamental qualities that the economy will acquire in the new civilization is **more subjective** production, a quality whose meaning we can understand from the new structure of knowledge and science described in previous chapters. The subjectivity to which I refer is the natural result of the act of placing the person and her/his fulfillment not only as the end product of the economy that is fulfilled in the process of consumption, but also as the origin and source of the production process of goods and services in the economy.

In the modern capitalist and statist economy, resources and production factors are considered in their external objectivity, and are in fact treated as things, or as purely material productive forces, quantifiable and measurable in monetary terms. Only jobs intend to and partly manage to keep some of the personal qualities, but jobs are also contracted and treated as something material, as 'labor force'.

In the new economy resources and production factors are recognized - from a new comprehensive science of diversity, subjectivity and values - in their condition as human energy and information, involving all the subjectivity they contain.

The labor force is the capability of production using the physical and mental capacities of the workers; it is an exercise of hands, conscience and willingness.

Technology is not in the technical artifacts, which are objective, but beyond them; it lies in the ability of invention, innovation and problem solving that people recognized for their theoretical and practical knowledge have.

Management is decision-making by those persons responsible for the organizations and processes.

Funding is the ability to obtain credit that people have on the basis of their trustworthiness to meet the commitments they make.

Even the material and inputs have a subjective dimension, in terms of their care, their maintenance, their ownership and use by people.

And obviously what we call the C Factor or community factor is subjective, since comes from the union of conscience, will and emotions towards the shared goals in a human group.

As soon as all these 'productive factors' are not treated as things and are conceived and recognized as actions taken by individuals, the economic units, the companies where they operate will be configured as organizations of active subjects, and their production processes will be understood and organized as the coordination of a coherent group of activities.

Thus **creating a business and making it grow is not so much combining and organizing a number of objective factors, but rather deploying a series of human actions, combining a series of verbs; the 'doing' of workers, the 'knowing' of the technologists, the 'deciding' of the managers, the 'believing' of the funders, the 'having' of the**

contributors of the means of production, and the 'uniting' of the community.

Production thus conceived and executed, oriented to 'good consumption', and organized in these creative, independent and supportive ways must be sustained over time and reproduced. This leads us to consider other important issues that i will examine in the following chapters.

XXXIV.

Will there be markets, money and profits in the new economy?

Realizing the injustices and inequities that occur in the market, the excessive importance attached to money and the exacerbation of the search for profits by companies and individuals, many have imagined the possibility and desirability of an economy that functions without money, without a market and without profits. Is it possible that markets, money and profits should not be in the new civilization?

The analysis of the causes of the injustices, inequities and moral distortions of the modern economy, and reflection on ways to organize the distribution of wealth, production and consumption in a fair and caring society take us in another direction, which is not that of imagining an economy without markets, money and profits. First let us consider the market.

We must consider that the market is not an invention of capitalism and is not identified with it; markets have existed since the dawn of history and have been present in all great civilizations. The truth is that the market exists because nobody, no person, family, community or country is self-sufficient to provide themselves with everything they need, and because the skills and resources are socially and geographically distributed, making it necessary to exchange resources, goods and services between different individuals, families, organizations, communities and countries. In fact, the market is an expression of the fact that we need each other and we work for each other.

As families, communities and countries, we are not independent and disconnected islands. The market is one of the ways we relate to individuals and groups in order to satisfy our needs, and make more efficient use of the capacities and available resources which are spread socially and scattered in different regions the world,

In this sense, the market is an integrator of society. And in the context of trade, by operating in the market each individual, community, organization and country, each with its resources and capabilities producing goods and services to meet the needs of others, individuals, organizations and communities deploy and increase our creativity, autonomy and solidarity.

Thus the factor which generates the inequality and exploitation is not the market itself, but rather its current capitalist and statist configuration. This is especially true in financial speculation, in which the process of enrichment is generated and reproduced separately from all useful economic activity.

This brings up the question of money. Will the money be the root of all evil? Do the distortions that lead to the concentration of wealth and widespread poverty arise from use of money in the market? In fact, some believe that we need to return to barter, reciprocity and exchange without money as ways to reach a human and socially just economy.

But money is not the cause of social injustice, although we can identify the source of many problems and inequities in the capitalist and statist mode of the circulation of money. In reality money is one of the greatest inventions of mankind; it has been improving for centuries and is very useful.

Although the current movements that promote exchange and reciprocity without money have provided valuable experiences due to the solidarity, creativity and autonomy they teach, the truth is that barter poses serious problems of efficiency and justice; it is difficult to perform because it requires every time the empirical coordination of the decisions of each bidder with those of each offerer; it only allows the exchange of physical goods in reduced areas and it is often unfair, because it has no mechanism for measuring the value of goods and services that are exchanged .

Money solves these problems by meeting socially necessary functions: It serves as the unit of measure of the value of the economic factors, goods and services. It is a universal medium of exchange which facilitates the coordination of the decisions of market participants, and it provides important information to make decisions through the price system.

And there are other problems that money solves. Individuals and societies need to ensure the future and have reserves of goods and assets for when they are needed. But accumulating resources and physical assets (wheat, bricks, etc.) would be very inefficient, because things may be damaged, lose value or be stolen. Money thus fulfills the function of serving as a medium to accumulate and store value, through savings, allowing us to access goods we need in the future based on the wealth produced in the past and present. Additionally, by loans and credit it allows the coordination in time the decisions of different economic agents, making what some save today (to spend tomorrow) available to those have needs today and will pay for them later.

However, similar to what happens in the market, the capitalist organization and functioning of money distorts it, affecting negatively each and every one of its functions, producing gross injustices and imbalances. This leads us to the issue of profit and earnings. Indeed, obtaining returns or earnings, also known as profit, has been questioned by those who want a fair and equitable economy; they have proposed as a solution an economy with non-profit economic activities and companies. This is due to the observation that the huge profits obtained by businessmen, speculators and others are the source of the enrichment of some and the impoverishment and marginalization of many.

But it must be emphasized that earning by itself is not the cause of the imbalances and economic and social inequities. Generating earnings and profits occurs because economic activity creates value, that is, that the product of the activity (the goods and services produced) is worth more than the resources and factors used in production. In other words, the **outputs** of economic activity are greater than the **inputs**, or more simply, the benefits outweigh the costs.

Economic activity creates value; the utility or profit is the difference between the value of the inputs and the value of the products. If there were no benefit and creation of value, economic activity would be mere reproduction of what exists, there would be no reason for creativity and innovation, and living would become stagnated. Again, the problem is not profit, but the capitalist mode in which the economic value generated is produced and how it is distributed.

Thus we must identify exactly where is the origin of distortions experienced by the market, money and profit in modern economy, and then discover the new ways that the market, money and profits may be organized in the economy of the new civilization.

These are the questions that will be addressed in the following chapters. But before turning to them let's get from this an important and crucial conclusion: **many of the central and more widespread ideas about economy that have circulated among those who have fought and are fighting for a fairer, more supportive and equitable society have not been based on an accurate understanding of the market, money and profits**. And consequently, when it has been postulated that a good economy must be a non-profit economy with no market and no money, either the goal or the type of economy to be built was wrong.

This has been caused by not having reached autonomy in the criticism of the present and in the conception of the changes necessary, which have remained subordinate to the separation and antagonism of capitalism and statism. From a new structure of knowledge, from a comprehensive economic theory, we must develop a new project for a good economy, appropriate for a new and superior civilization.

XXXV.

How will money and the financial system be in the new civilization? Community, national and global money.

The capitalist market is unfair, unbalanced and inequitable because wealth and power are highly concentrated. Power and wealth put those who have them in a position to make unequal exchanges, always giving less than they receive, which implies unjustified profit, entails the concentration of wealth and power in few hands, and leads to poverty, marginalization and exclusion of large social groups.

The concentration of wealth and power arise and accrue to the extent that economic gains are made at the expense of workers and consumers, and are predominantly to remunerate the capital and the State. In capitalist enterprises the companies take the profits directly, and then the State and its bureaucracies do so indirectly, by setting high taxes on consumption and income of individuals and businesses. And above and beyond the profits that are generated in the production and distribution process, banks and speculators obtain extraordinary profits because of the way in which money is currently issued and circulated in society.

Money is issued by the State and the banks reproduce and amplify it, causing it circulate in large and growing proportions outside the processes of production and consumption for which money should be used. Controlling the monopoly of issuing money, States often have emitted it inappropriately, generating inflationary processes in which the issuing State appropriates of a portion of the value of the money in circulation. In addition, when money is loaned at interest high rates its sole possession provides high profits, generated by a sequence of activities and processes of financial speculation, which involve a large and increasing appropriation of the wealth produced in the real economy.

The points that must be addressed to resolve these problems and inequalities are thus:
1. Organize the creation of money in a fair and just way.
2. Build an economy in which earnings go to those who produce them and are not produced at the expense of third parties.
3. Construct a market in which interchanges occur efficiently and with equity, without enriching some at the cost of others.

All this requires profound changes both in thought and economic science in the organization and practical functioning of the economy.

First of all a monetary system must be organized in which money is not depreciated by inflation, nor made scarce by an interest rate above what is strictly necessary. This requires creating a financial system in which depositors do not lose the value of their savings, but do not increase them by merely having money, and in which loans are granted at an interest rate sufficient to remunerate the financial service and to cover risks, but that does not lead to speculative processes which run independently of production and consumption. In these circumstances money will meet its five major functions with full efficiency and justice.

Thus we must ask: how money and the financial system should be structured in the new civilization? The first step will be a change in the issuers of money. At present States currently exercise the monopoly of issuing money; which they channel into circulation through banks organized by businesses. This corresponds, obviously, to the close association between business and the State in modern societies, which sustain each other and reach agreements.

However, in the new civilization, corresponding to the processes of emergence of local instances on one hand and planetary unity on the other, I predict that we will see a plurality and variety of local and community currencies appear, and also the creation of a universal currency in which trade is conducted internationally and globally.

Local and community currencies will be able to organize exchanges within cooperative, organized and supportive groups of people, in which locally available resources are appraised and allocated, in which the goods and services produced are distributed according to the needs that can be met at the level of intermediate organizations.

The single world currency will serve to organize and conduct international trade surpassing the current imperialist situation, where a few powerful States control the global financial system, and impose unequal terms of trade and exchange rates on other countries that inevitably favor the State issuers of the international currencies.

As a consequence of the emergence of new currencies at the community and world levels, national currencies may continue to serve for trade and finance within the States that recognize these currencies; but national currencies must also undergo decisive changes to avoid the disastrous events of devaluation and inflation that have characterized them throughout modern times.

Organizing the creation of these various currencies and their circulation through financial systems, so that they fulfill properly and efficiently the five major functions mentioned, is a technical issue not difficult to resolve. Indeed, this may be achieved by a relatively simple set of criteria and standards that ensure against inflation and inappropriate emissions, establishing emission quantities and interest rates commensurate with the demands of the real economy and preventing financial speculation. With these criteria and standards, production and consumption would not be forced to grow, as at present, just to meet the demands of the financial system, rather than being oriented towards the satisfaction of human needs.

But it is one thing to identify and understand the criteria and norms of a fair and efficient monetary and financial system, another to implement it in practice. Indeed, establishing the criteria and standards that regulate the creation and circulation of money in the new economy is only possible if associated with them informed, free and consensus agreements are reached among the economic actors who will be involved in the corresponding circuits, that is in the levels corresponding to the circulation of local and community currencies, national currencies and the single world currency for trade and international finance.

These participatory, informed and consensual arrangements are essential, because in the end currency is based on the trust and credibility of those who use it as a unit of measurement, a means of exchange, as means of saving, as credit and as a medium for the organization of economic activity over time.

Each one of these important and indispensible economic functions is based on trust and credibility that the currency generates for those who use it, and this trust and credibility can only be obtained in an effective and stable way when those who use it know exactly how it is issued, how it circulates, in what quantities, and what are the conditions in which it is used by the different actors in the economy Additionally, these actors will have participated in and have freely and knowingly agreed to the regulations which govern, guarantee and watch over the compliance of these criteria, rules and regulations.

When the economy has these three types of money -- local, national and world -- and their operation fulfills their duties properly, one of the most important causes of inequities we see in capitalist and statist economies will disappear. The exchanges between people, between companies and between countries will not be distorted by financial speculation or abusive exchange rates.

Initial steps in this direction are currently underway. At the local and community level there are creative experiences called 'complementary currencies', which are a real beginning of the creation of a new local financial and monetary system. These experiments are not always organized with the criteria and standards appropriate to operate efficiently; but the necessary learning process is occurring in the experimentation and reflection on the experiences themselves, which will lead to progressive improvement in their performance.

There are also more and more voices calling for the creation of a global currency which would function as the exchange medium in trade and international finance, as well as processes to improve the issue and circulation of national currencies in some countries.

These represent only the beginning of changes that must be very profound, that I will continue to examine in the next chapter.

XXXVI.

What are profits, how do they occur and how should they be divided in a fair and solidarity economy?

I affirm that one of the causes of the concentration of wealth and inequality in the modern economy lies not in the fact that earnings and profits occur, but rather in the amount of those profits, how they arise, and in which ways that they are apportioned. In the new economy earnings and gains will occur differently, and will be apportioned in a fair and supportive way. To understand both what is happening in today's economy and what we can conceive in a new economy, we need to analyze what is value and how value is created in the economy.

I assume that goods and services have a 'production value', given by the energy and information involved in their production. This 'production value' of goods and services has two components, one is the value of production factors that are transferred to goods or services produced, which is the cost, effort or sacrifice of the individuals who participate in the production; the other component is the value created by the

184

activity of producing the good or service. Since there is a creation of value, the product is 'worth' more than the cost of its production. It is this 'creation of value' which justifies that producers strive to perform productive activities.

Both components of the 'production value' have been 'incorporated' in goods and services by the activity of all subjects who participated in their production. Thus all goods and services produced contain some of the 'doing' of workers, the 'knowing' of the technicians, the 'have' of those who contributed the material, the 'decision' of the managers, the 'belief' of the financers and the 'union' of the productive community.

By all these activities the participants transferred to the products energy and information that they possessed, understood as forces or factors of production; but what occurs is not a simple 'zero-sum' transfer of value (in the sense that what was in the factors previously is equivalent to what is produced in the products), because with their activities the producers create new value which is incorporated in the product. In synthesis, the value of a product - its 'production value' - is the result of energy and information that those involved in the production spend and sacrifice to produce it, plus the value they create by their productive activity.

The value generated in production is transferred to consumers who use the goods and services to meet their own needs. In the hands of consumers products acquire a 'use value', which consists of the utility they provide or that can be extracted from the energy and information in the goods and services when they use them to satisfy their needs.

However, when production and consumption of goods and services are performed by the same person or group, the

185

'production value' and 'use value' are naturally compensated, those who produced the value use it to their own benefit. This is what happens in production for self-consumption.

But if producers and consumers are different people, an exchange between them is necessary; consumers must compensate the producers for the value they have provided with the products and services. This is what happens normally in the market, establishing an exchange between producers and consumers, using money as the unit of measure of value and as a universal medium of exchange. The amount of money involved in the exchange is often called the 'exchange value'.

For the exchange to take place, both participants, the producer and the consumer, must perceive that the value of what they obtain corresponds to the value of what they deliver, and that it is beneficial to both to make the exchange. Indeed, producers transfer the product only if they feel that the 'exchange value' (that they receive) corresponds to the 'production value' (that they give); that is, if it compensates for the cost incurred and the value created. In turn consumers pay the 'exchange value' only if they perceive that it corresponds to the 'use value' that the product has for them, that is, that the benefit or utility that the product provides will compensate for its cost.

This equation between 'production value', 'exchange value' and 'use value' is not essentially altered when commercial intermediaries operate between producers and consumers, because the intermediary is also a service provided to both the producer and the consumer, whose value must be compensated, so that the intermediary, the producer and the consumer all benefit.

Nor does it change the equation when the compensation of the 'production value' of the producer is not paid by the consumer but by the State or another entity that for benevolence or another reason provides the 'use value' of goods or services to the beneficiary. What happens in this case is that the producer gets the 'production value' and the consumer gets the corresponding 'use value'; the 'exchange value' is assumed by the State or by a third party benefactor. It is thus another form of intermediary between producers and consumers, which also has a value that someone pays.

In either case, it is only fair is that the 'production value', the 'use value' and the 'exchange value' be equivalent, because when they are equivalent the producer's profit corresponds to the value that he/she has created in productive activity. But in practice the equation can be distorted in 3 possible ways:

1. The 'exchange value' may be greater than the 'production value', which implies that the producer makes an unjustified profit at the expense of the consumer who pays more than the product is worth.

2. The 'exchange value' may be less than the 'production value', which implies that it is the consumer who makes an unjustified profit at the expense of the producer, that is, the product is obtained for less than it is worth.

3. The intermediary (of whatever kind) may appropriate a greater portion of the value than she/he deserves for the service, harming both the producer (who gets less) and consumer (who pays more) than they should.

There is an additional cause of gross distortions, which has a different explanation. The profit, which is the expression of the value created in production, is the result of the joint action of all persons and factors involved in production. The ideal form would be that each person and factor involved in the creation of the value participates also in the results, so that the value created is shared among all in proportion to what each has done and contributed. But if one of the persons who participate in the production receives more than he/she contributes, this person will be appropriating what corresponds to the other participants.

This is precisely what happens in the capitalist economy, in which those who provide the capital appropriate a very high percentage of the 'production value' at the expense of the people who provide the other factors, especially at the expense of workers and the community or Factor C, who receive less than what has been their contribution.

The cause of this appropriation is that companies in the capitalist economy are constituted in such a way that the capitalists - the owners of the financial factor and the material means of production - are the owners of companies and get all the profits generated, while those who provide the factors labor, technology, management and Factor C, since they are not part of the company but outside it, are hired with fixed salaries and do not participate in the profits they contributed to generate.

In a just and supportive economy companies will be organized through partnership and cooperation among all those who contribute the factors, that is, among those who perform the various activities involved in production. All are entitled to share in the profits obtained as an expression of the value created by all. And profits are distributed among them according to agreed criteria, implying that each one may receive payment for their rightful contributions and what they contributed to the creation of the value.

Having profits distributed fairly and equitably and the 'production value', 'exchange value' and 'use value' equivalent depends not only on how companies are organized, but also and mainly on how the market is structured. This is what I will examine in the next chapter.

XXXVII.

Is a fair market possible? What is a democratic market? How can we democratize the market?

We have seen that the market is a necessity: without the market people and communities could not subsist or develop. I also affirm that the market is a social fact that exists because individuals, communities and countries need each other, and because we work for each other. To participate in the market we must "make ourselves useful" to others, either through our work, by providing goods and services or by providing information and making available our "knowhow" and our organizational and entrepreneurial skills.

Although the market brings us together, it also separates us and brings us into conflict. In the market we reveal our social nature, but also our individuality, our personal interests and our selfishness. It is trade which constitutes the market; in an exchange we come with something we are willing to offer, and we are looking for something that others have. We exchange something for something else, and in this exchange each wants to receive as much as possible while giving as little as possible. Thus we find each other in the market reach an agreement, even though we have different and sometimes conflicting interests.

Since the exchange takes place when both parties are content with what they give and receive –otherwise reciprocal transfers do not occur- one might expect that in exchanges the parties transfer assets of equal value; that exchanges in the market are "equivalent for equivalent." This would be the situation where the 'production value', the 'exchange value' and the 'use value' are equivalent.

But we saw that in practice it is not like this, and that in exchanges it often happens that some win and others lose. Why is this? For the simple reason that in terms of trade people and companies use their market power, their commercial power. This "power" is given by a number of factors, including knowledge and access to information, negotiation skills, the different intensity with which each needs what the other has, the differences in wealth each has, the capacity to convince and deceive, and so on.

These differences of power give rise to tendencies toward concentration of wealth in the market. Indeed, if trade relations are unequal, the powerful triumphing over the weak in every price, the result is that power and wealth are constantly concentrated, while relative poverty is accentuated. It is worth asking whether trade must be like this, or more precisely, under what conditions the market could function without increasing existing inequalities.

Economists have answered yes, but only if the market could work under conditions of "perfect competition". That is, where economic agents do not have "market power", where there is equal opportunity for all, full transparency of information, open access (i.e. there are no barriers to the entry of new players for any type of activity), atomization of the participants (that is, all participants are small, no one monopolizes any activity), flexibility and full mobility (that participants can move from any activity to any other without barriers that hinder the movement), only then will exchanges be between equals and nobody will be able to profit unduly at the expense of others.

However, such conditions of "perfect competition" exist only in theoretical models. Indeed, the very concept of 'perfect competition' is based on a misunderstanding of what the market is, because it is conceived as an "automatic mechanism" that works independently of the will of the people. But the market is not this; it is the result of the activity of individuals and groups, of more or less conscious and voluntary decisions economic agents, who put into it their interests and passions, their selfishness and generosity, their pettiness and grandeur, their capabilities and limitations, their strengths and weaknesses. In the market people and all economic agents compete, each seeking to achieve a greater share of the wealth. To achieve this they organize, form alliances, exert influence on political powers, they use the media, produce misleading advertising, control and subordinate people, etc. Quite the opposite of an "automatic mechanism", the market is a 'balance of social forces'.

Because of all this, markets may be structured with greater or lower levels of competition or monopolist control, with different degrees of concentration or dispersion of power, and that is the determining factor of the degree of fairness and justice that exists in them. Since markets are constructed socially and reflect the historical relationship of social forces, a market may be more or less democratically organized. It may be democratic or oligarchic, depending on the degree of concentration or social dissemination of power that exists in the society. This is why I claim that "perfect competition" is an erroneous concept, since it neglects the fundamental fact that those who participate in the market always try to make their power count in trade.

In any case, it is easy to understand that what is closest to the theoretical condition of 'perfect competition' is what I called a "democratic market", that is, an economic organization in which power and wealth are socially distributed, disseminated throughout society, and where no one has monopolist or highly concentrated powers.

When the market is democratic, the profits of the various economic agents tend to agree with their efforts and contributions to the creation of the values, consumers pay fair prices for goods and services, workers receive the value of what they produce and there is not exploitation of some by others. Also, in this case, profits are generated and distributed with equity and justice, and the market strengthens its democratic organization.

Similarly, for the market to be democratic it is essential that the conditions must allow money - the three types of money required – to fulfill fully its five major functions, without distortion. And if money is thus created and circulated, the market will strengthen its democratic functioning.

I conclude that a new economy requires a fair and democratic market; constructing it is a fundamental part of creating a new civilization. The project is not an economy without a market, with no earnings and no money, but rather an economy with fair, legitimate and fairly distributed profits and efficient undistorted money. Achieving this is a process, as is the entire creation of a new civilization. The task is then, at this level, the progressive democratization of the market.

This democratization of the market implies advancing along a path that may be conceived as the practical creation of the theoretical assumptions of a democratic market: establish genuine equality of opportunity; make information available and develop the capacity to understand and use it; eliminate barriers to the access to resources, goods and services; allow full flexibility and mobility of market participants; reduce the power of large companies and facilitate the activities of small companies; organize associative enterprises in which profits are made and distributed fairly; and create local, national and global money in conditions that make them function efficiently and equitably.

But there is still more to understand and plan for a new and better economy. For although the market, money and business work perfectly, there are still economic problems to face. We will see this in the next chapter.

XXXVIII.

The role of State and of the economy of solidarity, work and communities. How much market, how much State and how much solidarity economy?

The democratization of the market, with all we saw that it implies, is the most important for the distribution of wealth to be fair and equitable. But having the most fair and democratic market does not solve all problems. There are basically two major economic areas in which the market is not sufficient, even if its operation is fully democratic, that require the action of two other major sectors and circuits of economic distribution, which are public and State economies, and the solidarity and community economies.

A first issue that the market and the exchanges themselves cannot solve is that, since the access to resources and goods and services in the market is through trade, one can only participate in the market to the extent that one has something to offer, and those who have little or nothing to offer do not have access to the goods and services needed to survive and meet basic needs. Thus the market excludes those who have no assets to exchange, and those who have, but cannot find others willing to pay for them. Thus a proportion of individuals and social groups are excluded from the market; the poor, orphans, the elderly, the disabled, the sick, the less skilled workforce, those with very little knowledge, etc. For this reason the market cannot be the only means of distribution of wealth in any society, because it would imply the death of countless people. Everyone has the right to live and fulfill their basic needs. The basic needs of those individuals and groups who cannot meet them by using their skills, their resources, their knowledge and their work should be solved outside the trade market, and society must be aware of this and organize the means to solve this problem. The needs of these people must be met first by their families, friends and by their communities, also with the support of donations from other generous individuals and organizations, and ultimately by the State, according to the principle of subsidiarity.

Another issue that the market and exchanges cannot solve is the production of so-called 'public goods and services' to which all members of the community have free access, their use by some not excluding their use by others. These public goods and services are usually designed to meet needs that are common to all members of a community or to benefit everyone, for example, the courts of justice, care of the environment, national defense, public order, streets and roads, parks and museums, public television, statistical services, certain levels of education and health that all citizens should have, regulation and control of production, trade, finance and several more.

The reason that the market cannot organize production, distribution and consumption of these 'public goods', is that individuals who benefit from their 'use value' are not willing to pay the corresponding 'production value', because access to them is free and can be had without incurring any cost. And if some were willing to pay, they would have to bear a high cost, paying for those who do not want to pay. Thus for these goods and services to be produced, their 'production value' must be assumed by the State, or by someone who represents the beneficiary group and can impose duties or taxes that finance them.

Modern economy been considered and established that the State must address these two great issues that the market cannot resolve - that of those excluded from the market and that of 'public goods and services'. The State addresses these needs by establishing a non-commercial distribution circuit, not based on trade but on taxation and distribution. On one hand the State centralizes the collection of money and resources by several duties and taxes paid compulsorily by people and businesses. On the other hand it distributes resources, goods and services through public expenditure and various allowances and subsidies.

But in fact modern states have been growing in size and economic functions consistently over many decades. There are two fundamental reasons for this growth; the proportion of the population that is excluded from the market is increasing, and the number and variety of needs that are satisfied with goods and services that fall under the classification of 'goods and public services' has been steadily increasing. These are the same phenomena we discussed when we dealt with consumption, which we saw as one of the dynamics that produce consumerism, along with the increase in the demands and rights that the populace requires from the State.

But there are serious problems with the growth of State. This is caused by the clamor for the State to meet the needs of the population and to provide more and more public goods and services; since those who obtain benefits this way do not feel or perceive the costs of producing these goods and services, which are assumed by society as a whole, it appears to them as something abstract, somewhat foreign and exterior. A consequence of this tendency is that, while the amount of the population that meets their needs in this way increases, the number of people who develop their skills and motivation to produce and create value decreases.

The result is that instead of creating conditions for greater equality, it is generating a growing split between fewer and fewer independent producers and increasingly dependent consumers. The equality that was thought to be achieved by increasing the taxes of the former and the benefits of the latter is more apparent than real. Although their levels of access and consumption of goods and services has become more similar, they increasingly drift apart in their levels of development of skills and resources.

Is there a solution? What would be the way to solve these problems in the new economy?

The real solution to these two problems, if you want a fair, efficient and equitable economy, is the creation and development of a third economic sector, we may call the economy of solidarity, labor and communities. Establishing this new economic sector between the market economy and the State economy will have significant impacts on the solution of the two major economic problems we are analyzing.

Regarding the first issue, this solidarity economy reduces exclusion and marginalization from the market, and allows the reintegration of many who are currently excluded and marginalized. It does not do this by generating passiveness of the recipients of public benefits, but rather by activity and enhancement of the capabilities that creative, autonomous and supportive producers and consumers have.

This supportive economy can also take charge of a significant share of common or general needs that are currently met with so-called 'public goods'. The way to do this is to have local communities take responsibility for providing those parts of the public goods that are used exclusively by the members of these communities. Because in reality, many of the 'public goods' to which all members of society at large theoretically have free access, in fact meet needs that are only of those of local or minor communities.

To meet the needs of environmental health, public protection, entertainment and recreation, health, education and others, there are many goods and services which are used locally and can be provided locally. Instead of paying taxes to the State to provide them, the participants of these organized communities could allocate those resources to provide 'public goods' needed locally. And by establishing a closer proximity between the beneficiaries of 'public goods and services' and the group or collective that assumes the costs of providing them, these "public goods" will be more tailored to the real needs of that community, and will also be taken care of better by those who employ them.

As an additional effect of all this, local communities will strengthen and develop their capabilities to solve their own problems and needs, instead of always delegating authority and expecting everything to come from higher authorities which wind up exercising power over them. This is also coherent and consistent with the dynamics of the new politics, as we have seen.

I thus conclude this reflection on the new economy, noting that it is best to have a pluralistic economy consisting of three economic sectors; the trade market, the public and State economy, and the economy of solidarity, work and communities. The best size for each of the three sectors - the trade market, the public sector and supportive sector - cannot be determined generally, but must correspond to the social, cultural and political conditions of each country and each place. But it is important to have a balance among them, bearing in mind that when a sector is constructed internally in a democratic and efficient manner, its size may be greater without adversely affecting society.

A highly concentrated trade market sector that generates a lot of poverty and exclusion will require a larger size of the State. A State which concentrates too many functions and assumes the responsibility for an excessive amount of the needs of a growing percentage of the population will generate an atrophied market of exchanges and solidarity, which will tend to generalize the dependence and poverty. A widely developed solidarity and democratic sector means that the State and commercial sectors of the economy are balanced, sized to the genuine contributions they can make to human and social development without encouraging consumerism and the unsustainable growth in resource use and environmental deterioration as occurs at present.

With these ideas we put an end to the analysis of the new economy, and approach a summary of the reflections and the conclusion.

XXXIX.

Ethics and spirituality which are committed to personal development and transformation of the world, seeking to evolve to higher forms of knowledge, consciousness and life.

Modern civilization is crumbling, slowly but inexorably. Institutions which guarantee order and social harmony are losing credibility and citizen support. States are restricted in their ability to conduct and coordinate the interests of different social groups and to solve problems that affect society. The economy is showing an inability to create jobs, to maintain social welfare levels previously achieved, and to prevent increased poverty, depletion of several key resources and environmental degradation. Ideologies and social sciences do not provide answers and viable solutions to these problems, and lose their ability to deliver projects that channel the concerns and demands, and in the context of the crisis multiply social unrest.

Awareness of these problems is spreading, which is a plus; but the outrage, protests and social mobilizations resulting from the expansion of awareness of the crisis are only expressions and manifestations of the crisis itself, which instead of resolving it actually enhance and accelerate it, since they do not lead to effective solutions. As long as these protests persist in demanding that the State and the existing institutions provide the solutions to the crisis and expect that the same market agencies that caused the crisis will reverse themselves and solve it, these mobilizations will be operating in the paradigms of the perishing civilization perishes and sharing the same crisis. It is curious that the same institutions in which people no longer believe and that are indicated as the ones responsible for the crisis are demanded to resolve the crisis. This shows that people still mistakenly think that the state and the market are all-powerful.

The crisis will continue to deteriorate economic, political and cultural life, in a long process of decline of modern civilization, which will involve much suffering and will be very painful. Thus it is very important to understand that the task ahead is constructive, and we should avoid actions that tend to destroy what is left of the existing economic and institutional order. Its own dynamics are destroying it, and accelerating its demise will not favor the new civilization.

It is also important to understand that the already old modern civilization has many elements of permanent value, as mentioned above, which we should conserve and as elements in the new civilization. There would be grave consequences if these elements were lost in the crisis of the decaying civilization, and it would also be extremely serious if the capitalist market and state institutions stopped functioning before the foundations of a new economy and a new social order have been established.

To understand this, just imagine that one day we find that banks have stopped functioning. Soon supermarkets and businesses of all kinds would be closed, including those providing fuel for transportation. Industries would be paralyzed, as well schools and basic services such as water, electricity and health. Pillaging, looting and crime would be rampant, and could not be contained by what few institutions continued to function. If instead of all this occurring suddenly it should happen gradually over a period of a few years, these negative consequences would be also occur and gradually extend during those same years, unless replacement solutions could be developed during that time.

But it is completely unrealistic to believe that the collapse of modern civilization will by itself lead to the new civilization, new politics, new economy, new sciences, new education and new technologies. They will emerge only to the extent that they are created by specific individuals and groups who consciously and decisively produce them. We have also said repeatedly that a new economics, politics, culture and science are in fact being created; they are emerging at the initiative of creative, autonomous and supportive persons. But it must be said that these have be deployed quickly enough to anticipate the crisis of modern civilization and to be established promptly. This is not automatic; it is not guaranteed.

It must also be emphasized that **the contents and forms the new civilization will take are not predetermined, but will be what those of us who assume the task of initiating the creation of a new civilization as a personal project are able to create, disseminate and develop.**

Building a new civilization is the largest, most global, comprehensive and most radical change that we could conceive. This big change will depend on the activity of many autonomous, creative and solidary people, not the result of the confrontations and the militancy of some tightly organized groups. The great transformation will not be produced by a single great movement unified by ideology, but through an infinity of actions, small and large, some infinitesimal and others of universal dimensions, covering the broadest fields of human experience, actions and deeds made by millions of people, each in their own lives and in their particular and diverse contexts. But all will be oriented by a common perspective, whose guidelines have been outlined throughout this volume.

However, the historical experience of past civilizations teaches us that when a civilization collapses, causing social, economic and political disorder, institutional decay, civil unrest, poverty, famine and conflict; the groups that lay the foundations of the new civilization must seek to protect themselves against the aggressions they may suffer in the context of accelerated deterioration of civil coexistence. This is why it is **urgent** to begin the construction process of the new economics, the new politics and the new civilization, to advance as much as possible in their creation.

This is not said to scare, but we need to know that it takes a lot of spiritual and moral strength and deep convictions; this is what will allow the creation of the new civilization, overcoming the difficulties of having to deploy the creative process in an adverse context that could even become dangerous.

This leads me to consider, as a last and decisive aspect to be analyzed, the spiritual and moral issue. **All great civilizations in the history of mankind have had profound and strong spiritual and moral foundations, which in final analysis are**

those that give humans the ability to rise above their biological drives and to evolve freely and consciously towards higher stages of superior and transcendent civilization.

Ethics as theoretical thinking that guides to good living, to identify the minimal moral duties and the highest virtues, and ultimately to achieve the greatest possible happiness for all human beings, is an intellectual discipline which is also now in crisis and which it will be necessary to redesign and reconstruct. This crisis of ethics leads to a crisis of moral practice, behavior and habits, and this is one of the major obstacles to the creation of a new and superior civilization, which is why it is moving much more slowly than is needed and that we would like.

What seems to be required in this area is to develop at a theoretical level and to train ourselves in practical terms in an ethics of personal, social and environmental responsibility founded in the values of justice and solidarity. And in connection with such ethics, **to develop a spirituality human development, strongly committed to transforming ourselves and the world, seeking to evolve to higher forms of knowledge, consciousness and living**.

We have seen, I have said and reiterated throughout these presentations, that the creation of the new civilization calls everyone, and requires commitments of persons working in economics, politics, artistic and cultural creation, scientific research, education and communications. It must be emphasized that **the project of creating a new and higher civilization convenes and gives special responsibility to those who feel motivated, or believe they are called, or indeed are searching for what with different orientations and directions can be understood as spiritual development.**

205

Taking into account that unlike so many other human qualities and skills such as cognition, sports and communications, in which the potential is so different from person to person, spirituality appears as perhaps the only truly democratic human potential, meaning that we can all share it; it consists basically of the capacity to love: to love yourself, love others, to love nature, to love a superior Being.

This brings us to the last question which I address in the next and final chapter: how can we understand the idea of a 'new man', or a new 'human type' that could develop in the new civilization?

XL.

In what sense can we speak of a 'new man'?

At the beginning of these reflections on how to start creating a new civilization, I proposed that this involves the formation of a new 'human type', which I characterized as creative, autonomous and solidary.

This idea of a new 'human type' is easily associated with a 'new man', an idea with has expressed the aspiration that all religions have, and also the most important ideologies and modern political utopias. But what would this really be in our case? How can we conceive the idea of creating a new 'human type' for the new civilization? Would this mean changing human nature?

It is very important to clarify this issue, as many argue that the project of a just and united society or of a better civilization is unrealistic because it ignores human nature; that many people are naturally selfish and competitive individuals who put their interests and those of their small group members over the public interest or common good.

The first thing I can say about this is that human beings throughout history and around the world have formed very different assumed forms of being, thinking, relating and acting, and therefore the species human presents a great flexibility and plasticity.

This observation leads me to conceive of 'human nature' as a certain basic structure consisting of some general features and elements common to all people (regardless of the time, social organization, historical conditions, etc.); but it is a basic or 'essential' nature that remains open, and has the ability to take on other more complex features and forms that can lead it to evolve, to acquire other forms and structures, as **though it were a structure that wanted to be another structure.**

It may be more accurate to think of essential human nature as a basic primary structure on which other structures may be built, or on which a second 'nature can be established which can take different configurations.

I argue that consumer behavior and the individualistic and greedy behavior of individuals which is so widespread in modern civilization is not a direct and unique expression of 'human nature', but the manifestation of a sort of second 'nature' which was built on the first in the course of the formation and development of an economics and politics that needed it and which built it.

However, the formation and consolidation of the different collective modes of being and acting that have happened in history in a number of civilizations seems to have involved both elements of consciousness and will of the people themselves, and factors of coercion and dominion which imposed by force a way of being and acting that was spread socially.

Antonio Gramsci said, "So far all the changes in ways of being and living have occurred by brutal coercion, or through the domination of one social group over all the productive forces of society; the selection or "education" of persons adapted to new types of civilization, that is, to new forms of production and work, has happened with the use of unprecedented brutality." This statement of Gramsci may be unilateral and not recognize sufficiently different historical situations. But what is true is that almost always the masses have tended to be shaped by the dominating groups that have used different media, from coercion to propaganda, from education to politics, and even by certain forms of art, cinema, music, etc.

In any case, if we consider the development of a new, creative, autonomous and solidary 'human type', it seems essential to understand how the new second 'nature' could be designed and created, and what relation it would have with essential 'human nature'.

First of all, it is obvious that essential 'human nature' must be such as to allow second 'natures' to arise. Since this possibility does not seem attributable to other animal species, we may identify consciousness as a specific human feature, and more precisely rationality and freedom, as the base that makes possible the creation of second 'natures'. This free consciousness is what makes it possible for people to rise above their biological nature to a degree, or better yet, to take control of the direction of their own development and evolution. It is essential to be free to be able to differentiate and change, and to be rational in order to take control and define a direction of change, so that one can create a different 'structure', as we have also called the second 'nature'.

However, conscience and freedom are not enough to produce a human second 'nature'. Indeed, consciousness and freedom are attributes of individuals. But here we are talking about a second 'nature' that, while it may not involve all human beings, should at least include a large human population, because we are considering the dimensions of a civilization. Therefore, the second 'nature' must be 'social', but this time not imposed by force. Well, sociability is also a characteristic of 'human nature', like rationality and freedom. This means that a second 'nature' can be created socially, i.e. as a process of social construction that actively incorporates many individuals who associate, communicate, share a given rationality and the will to join a collective creative process.

But in fact we start with the current situation, in which human beings are more 'social' than 'free'. I mean that usually, and especially in economic and political activity, people today act strongly conditioned by the community of which they form part, and by the cultural context in which they grow and learn. Individual freedom is always manifested, but usually in small events in minor decisions, while in the main directions that historical and structural processes take, most follow the established directions, and act as 'masses'. Modern civilization needed and formed this.

At this point the reader will have already realized that creating a new and higher civilization consists, in the final analysis, in the creation of a new and higher second 'nature' in humans, starting with ourselves. This is possible due to essential 'human nature', since it derives from rationality and freedom, and due to the fact that we are 'social', and therefore able to build economic, political and cultural processes and organizations.

However, to **start** the creation of this new and higher second 'nature' based on essential 'human nature', it is necessary to separate from the current second 'nature', that old and inferior 'nature' that was imposed in modern civilization. To start creating a new second 'nature', is therefore necessary that at least some individuals achieve autonomy (due to their own rationality and freedom). These individuals, organized in networks and enhancing each other, will expand the new way of being and behaving, through the actions and processes we have been examining. But we must assume that the beginning of the creation of a new civilization is today, as it has been in the past, a process initiated by few, because few apply their freedom to the main directions of their lives and do not limit themselves to deciding on secondary issues in a socially established and predetermined framework,.

For us to begin creating in ourselves a new second 'nature' we must connect with our essential nature, making ourselves more free, rational and social. Only then can we become creative, autonomous and solidary. Unless we connect with our essential 'human nature' (hidden, suppressed by the current second 'nature'), we cannot start creating a new and superior second 'nature'. That is why the first step in the creation of the new is to "know thy self" and come to think with our own minds instead of participating in a passively assumed worldview which can only be old, created in the previous socially and culturally defined historical process, which has become habit.

We must establish intimate contact with our essential 'human nature'. But our 'human nature' key is hidden and suppressed by the second 'nature' that the statist and capitalist civilization has built into us, thus it is necessary to begin the conquest of autonomy from the second 'nature' and those ways of thinking and behaving that belong to the old current modern civilization.

This is a process of personal growth, which at its root is a process of spiritual development. But it must not remain locked within each person, but rather be expressed and projected to create a new economy, a new politics, new science, a new education and new forms of culture.

It is in the process of creating the new civilization that the 'new man' will be generated and disseminated socially; the creative, autonomous and supportive 'human type' of the new civilization. For it is through the conquest of autonomy, creativity development, and spreading of solidarity, that we will develop a new human second 'nature', superior to that we must leave behind like an old suit that is not worth mending.

Index

Manufactured by Amazon.ca
Bolton, ON